MW01121970

Control box   Title bar   Command button

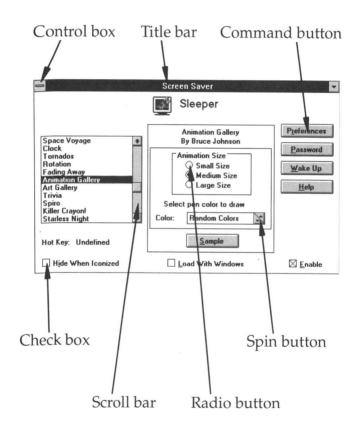

Check box   Spin button

Scroll bar   Radio button

The SYBEX Instant Reference Series

Instant References are available on these topics:

AutoCAD Release 11

dBASE

dBASE III PLUS Programming

dBASE IV Programming

dBASE IV 1.1

DESQview

DOS

DOS 5

Harvard Graphics 3

Harvard Graphics for Windows

Lotus 1-2-3 Release 2.3

Lotus 1-2-3 for Windows

Macintosh Software

Microsoft Word for the Macintosh

Microsoft Word for the PC

Norton Utilities 6

PageMaker 4.0 for the Macintosh

Paradox 3.5

PC Tools 7.1

Quattro Pro 3

Windows 3.1

Windows 3.0

Word for Windows, Version 2.0

WordPerfect 5

WordPerfect 5.1

WordPerfect 5.1 for Windows

Computer users are not all alike.
Neither are SYBEX books.

We know our customers have a variety of needs. They've told us so. And because we've listened, we've developed several distinct types of books to meet the needs of each of our customers. What are you looking for in computer help?

If you're looking for the basics, try the **ABC's** series. For a more visual approach, select full-color **Teach Yourself** books.

Learn Fast! books are two books in one: a fast-paced tutorial, followed by a command reference.

Mastering and **Understanding** titles offer you a step-by-step introduction, plus an in-depth examination of intermediate-level features, to use as you progress.

Our **Up & Running** series is designed for computer-literate consumers who want a no-nonsense overview of new programs. Just 20 basic lessons, and you're on your way.

SYBEX **Encyclopedias**, **Desktop References**, and **A to Z** books provide a *comprehensive reference* and explanation of all of the commands, features, and functions of the subject software.

Sometimes a subject requires a special treatment that our standard series don't provide. So you'll find we have titles like **Advanced Techniques, Handbooks, Tips & Tricks,** and others that are specifically tailored to satisfy a unique need.

You'll find SYBEX publishes a variety of books on every popular software package. Looking for computer help? Help Yourself to SYBEX.

For a complete catalog of our publications:

SYBEX Inc.
2021 Challenger Drive, Alameda, CA 94501
Tel: (510) 523-8233/(800) 227-2346 Telex: 336311
Fax: (510) 523-2373

SYBEX

SYBEX is committed to using natural resources wisely to preserve and improve our environment. This is why we have been printing the text of books like this one on recycled paper since 1982.

This year our use of recycled paper will result in the saving of more than 15,300 trees. We will lower air pollution effluents by 54,000 pounds, save 6,300,000 gallons of water, and reduce landfill by 2,700 cubic yards.

In choosing a SYBEX book you are not only making a choice for the best in skills and information, you are also choosing to enhance the quality of life for all of us.

Norton Desktop™ for Windows™, Version 2.0 Instant Reference

Second Edition

Sharon Crawford
and
Charlie Russel

SYBEX ®

San Francisco • Paris • Düsseldorf • Soest

Acquisitions Editor: Dianne King
Series Editor: James A. Compton
Editor: David Krassner
Technical Editor: Martin Moore
Word Processors: Ann Dunn and Susan Trybull
Book Designer: Ingrid Owen
Screen Graphics: Cuong Le
Typesetter: Ann Dunn
Proofreader/Production Assistant: Janet K. Boone
Indexer: Nancy Guenther
Cover Designer: Archer Design

Library of Congress Card Number: 92-81526
ISBN: 0-7821-1109-2

Manufactured in the United States of America
10 9 8 7 6 5 4 3 2 1

Acknowledgments

The authors wish to heartily thank Ann Dunn, Deborah Maizels, Janet Boone, David Krassner, Martin Moore, Dianne King, Gary Masters, Peter Dyson, Ingrid Owen, Nancy Guenther, and numerous others in and around Sybex. Our appreciation also to Robin Selder, Nancy Stevenson, and Robert Kerwin at Symantec.

All the above were a pleasure to deal with at every turn.

Table of Contents

Introduction

xv

Part One

An Overview of
Norton Desktop for Windows

Part Two

Configuring the Desktop

Part Five
The Norton Windows Batch Language

Part Six
The Fix-It Disk Programs

Appendix A
Installation

Appendix B

Configuring the Desktop in Version 1.0

Index

Introduction

Norton Desktop for Windows offers quick and elegant solutions to many of the problems that can plague users of Windows. In addition to Windows versions of the familiar Norton disk utilities, Norton Desktop for Windows includes features designed to bypass the File Manager and Program Manager, making Windows even easier to use.

Using the Drive Windows, you can move, copy, print, or even back up files with just a few mouse clicks. Quick Access allows you to set up groups and subgroups in ways that are completely independent of your DOS menu structure. These tools have no equivalent in Windows. The Norton Desktop for Windows package offers dozens of ways to configure your system to fit your specific work needs, and you can choose to use all of these or just a few. This book presents them all clearly and simply.

Instant Reference books are intended to provide quick access to all the functions of a program. In the case of Norton Desktop for Windows, so many options are available that it may take you a while to become familiar with them. The aim of this book is to give you, in brief form, the essential information that you will need to answer any questions that may come up while you are using the program. You need not be an experienced user of either Norton Desktop or Windows. Explanations for all of the terms used can be found in *A Quick Guide to Navigating the Desktop* in *Part One*. If you have not yet installed Norton Desktop for Windows, see *Appendix A: Installation* for a guide to installation.

HOW THIS BOOK IS ORGANIZED

The information in this book covers both Version 2.0 and Version 1.0 of Norton Desktop for Windows. *Part One: An Overview of Norton Desktop for Windows* includes definitions and descriptions of all the terms used in this book. Note that both Windows and Norton Desktop for Windows use the same names for the various buttons, boxes, and other parts of the interface.

Part Two: Configuring the Desktop covers the many configuration options for the desktop. Here you will learn how to change the way
Norton Desktop looks and behaves. In this section, Versions 2.0 and
1.0 are so diverse that the two versions must be treated separately.
The configuration options for Version 1.0 are in *Appendix B: Configuring the Desktop in Version 1.0.*

Part Three: Managing Files covers the File Management functions, including the Drive Windows, the highly useful substitute for the File
Manager in Windows. This is where you will find the commands
for copying, moving, deleting, and otherwise manipulating files.

Part Four: Tools and Utilities includes the calculators, the Desktop Editor
(Version 2.0 only), screen savers, a scheduling program, and numerous
utilities to save you time and ensure the safety of your work.

Part Five: The Norton Windows Batch Language covers the Batch Language, a powerful tool for manipulating your Windows environment.

Part Six: The Fix-It Disk Programs details the programs found on the
Fix-It Disk. These programs are valuable tools for rescuing errant
computers and their users.

Part One

An Overview of Norton Desktop for Windows

Norton Desktop for Windows can organize and facilitate every aspect of your work inside Windows. Version 2.0 includes many new tools and accessories as well as providing the means to adjust virtually every aspect of your computer's look, feel, and operation within the Windows environment.

For the most part, this book assumes that you are running Norton Desktop for Windows as your Windows shell (See *Appendix A* for information on installation options.) If you are not using Norton Desktop as a shell, you will need to open the Norton Desktop group and then select the Norton Desktop icon to reach the menus and functions that are described.

If you intend to use only the tools and utilities, you can decline to run Norton Desktop as your shell and just select specific tool icons from the Norton Desktop group as you need them for particular tasks.

Most functions in Norton Desktop for Windows, as in Windows, can be activated either from the keyboard or with a mouse. Instructions in this book will usually tell you to "select" or "click on" a given choice. This can be done with the mouse or by keystrokes to move the cursor.

USING THE KEYBOARD

You pull down menus by pressing the **Alt** key and the letter that is underlined in the menu name. When the menu is visible, you make your selection by keying in the letter that is underlined in the command name.

In a dialog box, the cursor appears as a dotted line outlining the choice. The cursor also appears as a vertical line in a text box. To turn a selection on or off, press the spacebar while the cursor outlines that choice. When the cursor is on a button, press ↵ to choose it. Inside a dialog box, the cursor can be moved using the ↑, ↓, ←, or → keys, as well as the **Tab** key.

USING A MOUSE

To click on an item, first position the mouse pointer over that item, then press and release the left mouse button once. Double-clicking means that you position the pointer and press the mouse button twice in rapid succession.

To drag an item, click on it and hold down the mouse button. When you move the mouse, you will see the item pulled along the screen. When you reach the place where you want the item to go, release the mouse button.

To select an item from a menu, click on the menu's name. While holding down the mouse button, move the mouse until it highlights the item you want, then release the button. You can also select an item from a menu by clicking once on the menu's name and once on the item.

To select multiple items from a list, such as a directory of files, you can use one of the following methods:

Shift-click selects contiguous items on a list. Hold the **Shift** key down and click on the first item you want. Keep **Shift** depressed, move to the last item, and click on it. The first, last, and all items between will be highlighted.

Ctrl-click selects noncontiguous items on a list. Hold down the **Ctrl** key while clicking on the items you want.

Version 2.0 also includes menu items to Select and Deselect files. See *Part Two, Drive Windows.*

MENUS

In the Norton Desktop there is a menu bar with the names of the menus at the top of the screen. Click on the name of the menu, and the listing will appear below it. By default, the program opens with the short version of the menus. To see the full listing you must select Configure ➤ Load Menu.

Menu names include other indications as to their functions. For example, an ellipsis (…) following a menu name signifies that choosing that item will open a dialog box with additional choices. A solid triangle after an item means that a submenu will appear when that item is highlighted.

Some menu items, such as the first four items under the View menu, are toggles. (A toggled item is alternately turned off and on each time you select it.) When you select one of these, a check mark will appear indicating that the function is on. When you click on the item again, the check mark will disappear and the function will be toggled off.

Functions that are dimmed are not available for use. For example, the Net Drive functions in the Disk menu are dimmed unless you are on a network.

BOXES AND BUTTONS

Everything you do in Norton Desktop for Windows must be done by means of various boxes and buttons. It may seem that there are many names for similar functions, but you should familiarize yourself with these names because they signify how the box or button can be used.

Browse Box   When you select a browse button, a browse box will open. It usually includes file, directory, and drive windows, so you can locate files whose exact name or location you may not remember. When you find and select the file and then click **OK**, the file's name will appear in the original dialog box. A double-click on the file's name will have the same result.

Check Box   A square box next to an item is a check box that can be turned on or off. To select that item, click on the square box. An X will appear to indicate that the item is toggled on. To turn the choice off, select the square box again and the X will disappear.

Speed-Search Box   A speed-search box is the quickest way to find a file or directory in a Tree Pane or File Pane. When you start typing the name of the file or directory, the speed-search box appears below the active pane and the cursor bar moves to highlight the first file or directory that matches the letters typed. When the cursor bar has moved to the file or directory you want, press ↵ to select it.

Tri-State Box   A tri-state box is just like a check box, except that it has three settings. If there is an X in the box, the option is turned on. If the setting is blank, the option is turned off. If the box is a solid gray, the program will disregard whether the option is on or off.

Text Box   A text box is a blank box where you key in text or numbers. Click anywhere in the text box and a blinking cursor will appear at the left side of the box. Begin keying in text at the cursor. To make a change in your text, press the **Backspace** key. Alternately, click and drag the mouse across the part of the text that you want to change to highlight it and press the **Del** key.

Drop-Down Box   A drop-down box is a text box with a choice already in it and a prompt button on the right side of the box. Click the prompt button, and the box will open downward and reveal other choices you can select.

Combination Box   A combination box looks and acts like a drop-down box, except that in addition to the choices provided, you can also key in your own choice.

Dialog Box   A dialog box is a small window that allows you to select the options available for the program or function chosen. The term dialog box is used often in Windows and refers to any box with user choices. Dialog boxes always appear when you choose a menu command that contains an ellipsis (…).

Control Box   The control box is at the upper left-hand corner of the main Norton Desktop window and all other windows and dialog boxes. It is a gray box with a slotlike mark. To see the Control menu, click on the control box.

Command Button   When selected, a command button causes the program to execute an action. Command buttons include **OK**, **Cancel**, **Select**, **Browse**, and so forth. They are rectangularly shaped and when they are selected, they appear to depress.

Help Button   A help button is available in most windows and dialog boxes. When you select this button, a screen will appear with information on the program or function you are using. These help screens operate like the Windows help screens. Consult your Windows documentation for more information on using the help system.

The Minimize and Maximize Buttons   At the upper right-hand corner of the Norton Desktop and of many program screens there are buttons with either up or down arrows and some buttons with both up and down arrows. A button showing both up and down arrows indicates that the window is at its maximum size; clicking on that button will reduce the window to its normal operating size. To minimize a window, select the button with a downward-pointing arrow. Note that a program that has been minimized remains open. To maximize the window, select a button with an upward-pointing arrow.

Prompt Button   A prompt button is located on the right side of a drop-down or combination box. It has a down-pointing arrow on it indicating that you can click to make more choices available.

Radio Button   Radio buttons function just like the selection buttons on a radio. Only one can be on at a time. To select one is to deselect any other. Usually, a radio button is round and when it is toggled on, its center darkens.

Spin Buttons   Spin buttons are divided diagonally with an up arrow in one corner and a down arrow in the other. Clicking on one corner or the other will cycle you through a loop of choices.

BARS

Bars appear on dialog boxes and other windows. The title bar, menu bar, and scroll bars provide information on the window's function and contents.

Title Bar   The title bar appears at the top of every window and box. The name of the program or dialog box is written there. To move a window, click on the title bar and drag the window to the location you choose. Double-click on the title bar to maximize the window.

Menu Bar   The menu bar is just below the title bar. Only the titles of available menus appear on the menu bar. When you select a menu name, a list appears with any currently unavailable items dimmed.

Scroll Bar   Whenever the information in a window will not fit into the available space, the window will have a scroll bar on its right edge. To move up or down in the window, click the up or down arrow. To move more rapidly, click and drag the slider box in the scroll bar.

Some windows will also have horizontal scroll bars that work in the same manner, except that they move from side to side.

ICONS

An icon is a miniature, graphic representation of a program, tool, file, or group. When a program is "iconized" it remains open on the desktop without taking up desk space. Simply click on a program's minimize button and it will continue to run while you are doing something else.

When you are ready to return to the iconized program, you can click it open again without having to search through a directory or key in instructions.

Drive Icons When Norton Desktop opens, you will see icons that represent your computer drives on the left side of the screen. The top two icons—the small disk drives—represent your A: and B: floppy-disk drives. Below these, there will be an icon for each of your hard drives. If you have a RAM drive or network drives, special icons for these will also appear. Click on these icons to open Drive Windows.

Program Icons When Norton Desktop for Windows starts, several icons representing the program tools appear on the right side of the screen. Icons representing programs also appear in all the group windows. Icons can be dragged from the group windows to the desktop where they will remain until selected and closed. Programs can be opened by double-clicking on the program icon.

Group Icons Group icons represent an entire collection of related applications. There are icons in the Quick Access window that each represent a group of programs.

WILDCARDS

Norton Desktop for Windows recognizes the following wildcard characters:

? represents a single character at the corresponding position.

* represents all the remaining characters in the field.

¦ represents one or zero characters.

Entries in this book specify those cases where wildcards cannot be used.

● EXAMPLES

BUDGET.PR? represents all files with the name BUDGET where the extension begins with the letters *PR*, but any character can be in the third position.

BUDGET.* represents all files with the name BUDGET with any extension.

¦¦**.PRN** represents all files with the extension PRN that also have two or fewer characters in their names.

Part Two

Configuring the Desktop

ASSOCIATING A FILE EXTENSION WITH A PROGRAM

When you associate a file name extension with an application, you can then select any file with that extension and the associated program will open automatically. Norton Desktop for Windows automates Windows' association of file extensions with programs.

To Add an Association

1.   Select File ➤ Associate.

2.   In the Extension text box, type in the three-letter extension, but do not include the period (.) in the extension. If you have already highlighted a file name in a Drive Window, its extension will appear in the box automatically.

3.   In the Associate With combination box, type in the program's full path name (including the extension) or .PIF file name, or select from the list of applications available. You can also use the Browse button to find the program's file name and path. If you use the Browse button, you can double-click on the file name, and the path and file name will appear in the Associate With box.

4.   Click on **OK**.

To Delete an Association

1.   Select File ➤ Associate.

2.   In the Extension text box, type in the extension you wish to delete. The associated program will immediately appear highlighted in the Associate With combination box.

3.   Select (None) from the list in the box. Click on **OK** to confirm the deletion or **Cancel** to abandon the change.

• **NOTES**   After you remove an extension from the list of associated files, you can no longer launch files with that extension from the desktop.

Norton Desktop for Windows does not allow wildcards in associated extensions. You must explicitly specify each extension that you wish to associate with a given program.

A particular extension can be associated with a single program only, but any program can have as many extensions associated with it as you need.

See Also   *Launch Manager/Launch List*

BUTTON BAR

The button bar at the bottom of the Drive Window can be omitted by deselecting the Display Button Bar option in the Configure Button Bar window, or it can be edited in various ways.

To Change the Button Command

1.   Select Configure ➤ Button Bar.

2.   Find the command you want on the Menu Item list and select it with the mouse.

3.   Click the button you want to assign the command.

4.   Select **OK** when you are finished. To make the change permanent, choose Configure ➤ Save Configuration or activate the Save Configuration on Exit check box in the Configure ➤ Preferences dialog box.

• **NOTE**   Select commands carefully. For example, the Menu Item list includes two items named *All*. One is from the Select menu and the other from the Deselect menu. Even though their names are the same, their functions are exactly opposite.

See Also   *Saving the Configuration*

To Edit a Button's Text

1. Select **Edit** in the Configure ➤ Button Bar dialog box.

2. In the Edit Button Bar dialog box, click on the text box of the button you want to modify and key in the new text. The program will beep if you attempt to enter too much text.

3. Click **OK** when you are finished.

● **NOTE**   Take care not to change the meaning of the button. Changing the text on the button changes only its appearance. The function of the button can be changed only by selecting another Menu Item in the Configure Button Bar window.

CONFIRMATION REQUESTS

You can do many things in Norton Desktop for Windows—some of which you may later regret. To protect yourself from various types of hasty acts, you can arrange for dialog boxes to ask for confirmation for potentially disastrous actions.

To Be Prompted for File Names

1. Select Configure ➤ Preferences.

2. From the Prompt for Filename box, choose the operations for which you would like a prompt.

3. Click on **OK** when you are finished.

● **NOTE**   The Prompt for Filename option works when you first select one or more files from a Drive Window and then choose the Edit, View, Print, or Delete functions. It is a precaution that allows you to change your mind before taking an action. If you don't want to be prompted, clear the check boxes.

To Select Confirmation Requests

You can choose to have dialog boxes pop up and ask for confirmation when certain potentially dangerous operations are attempted. To do this, follow these steps:

1. Select Configure ➤ Confirmation.

2. Click on the confirmation options you want.

3. Click on **OK** when you are finished.

● OPTIONS

Delete warns when you are deleting an unprotected file. If Erase Protect is on, the warning message will not appear, but you will still be asked to confirm the deletion.

Subtree Delete warns you about any operation involving the removal of a directory.

Replace warns you about any copy operation that involves overwriting another file. This box should *remain checked* because if you write over a file, the file will be lost and *not recoverable by any means.*

Mouse Operation opens a confirmation dialog box for all mouse operations that move, copy, or delete files.

Unassociated Print warns you when you try to print a file with no associated application. This will appear whether the File ➤ Print File command is used or the file has been dragged from a Drive Window to the Desktop Printer Icon. (Called *Unformatted Print* in Version 1.0.)

Exit Norton Desktop warns that you are about to exit Norton Desktop and requests that you confirm this choice.

CONTROL MENUS

Control menus appear when you click once on a desktop icon or when you click once on the control box (found in the upper-left corner of application windows.) An application window's Control menu can be reconfigured. A desktop icon's menu can only be turned on or off.

To Configure the Control Box Menus

1. Choose Configure ➤ Control Menu.

2. In the Configure Control Menu dialog box, check those items you want to appear on application Control menus.

3. Click **OK** when you are finished.

To Turn On the Drive/Tool Icon Control Menu

Drive icons and tool icons have Control menus that can be turned on and off. Desktop icons that represent files or applications have Control menus that are always on.

1. Select Configure ➤ Preferences.

2. Click on the **Advanced** button.

3. Select the Drive/Tool Icon Menu option box.

4. Click **OK** in both boxes when you are finished.

● OPTIONS

Click once on a drive or tool icon to see its Control menu.

Open opens the drive or starts the program.

Icon allows you to select another icon.

Label opens a dialog box where you can change the label that appears under the icon.

Close closes the drive or program and removes the icon from the desktop.

DESKTOP ICONS

The appearance of icons can be changed by selecting from the icons available in the Norton Desktop for Windows, or by designing your own icons using the Icon Editor.

To Select Tool Icons

1. Choose Configure ➤ Preferences.

2. In the Tool Icons box, check the boxes for the icons you want on the desktop. If you have more than one printer, click on the **Printers** button to choose the one you want associated with the Printer Icon. Up to four printers, including a fax machine, can be selected, and each printer will have its own icon.

3. When you have made your selections, click **OK**.

● **NOTE**   To reduce desktop clutter, you can choose not to create an icon for every printer that you might want to use. The full Printer Selection box is also available when you select File ➤ Print.

To Arrange Desktop Icons

Using the mouse to click and drag, you can place the tool icons anywhere on the desktop. To keep them at a distance from one another, turn on the Snap Desktop Items to Grid option box under Configure Preferences. To restore them to their original positions, take the following steps.

1. Select Configure ➤ Preferences.

2. Clear all the option boxes in the Tool Icons list and click **OK**.

3. Open the Configure Preferences dialog box again. Click on the option boxes for the tool icons you want. Then click **OK**. The tool icons selected will reappear in their original locations.

To Change an Icon Label

1. Click once on the desktop icon.

2. Choose Label from the Control menu.

3. Key in the label you want to appear on the icon.

4. Select **OK** when you are finished.

● **NOTE** The Drive/Tool Icon Control Menu option, found by choosing Configure ➤ Preferences (Advanced), must be switched on to change the icon or the icon label. This check box item is found by choosing Configure ➤ Preferences.

To Change a Desktop Icon

1. Click once on the desktop icon.

2. Select Icon from the Control menu.

3. The Choose Icon dialog box opens, as shown in Figure II.1. The path for the current icon is shown as the Default Icon File. For Alternate Icon Files, click on the

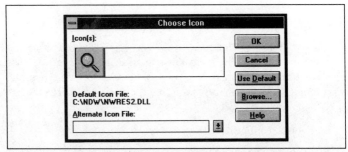

Figure II.1: The Choose Icon dialog box

prompt button or type the icon file name into the text box.
Select any of the files that appear for additional icons to
choose from.

4.   Choose an icon from the Icon(s) box or click on the **Use
Default** button to return to the item's original icon. Select
OK when you are finished.

● **NOTE**   The source files for icons will have one of seven possible extensions: .ICO, .NIL, .EXE, .DLL, .ICN, .ICL, or .IL. Therefore,
the Browse dialog box will show only files with these extensions.
However, not all files with these extensions will have icons in them.
If you select a new source file and the Icon(s) box turns up blank, it
means that the selected file contains no icons.

DRIVE WINDOWS

Drive Windows are the heart of Norton Desktop for Windows.
They replace the Windows File Manager, allowing you to copy,
move, delete, view, and find files easily with a button click or two.
By default, Drive Window buttons appear on the left side of the
desktop and include all available drives (including networked
drives); like most things in Norton Desktop for Windows, this is
configurable.

To Configure the Drive Icons

1.   Select Configure ➤ Drive Icons.

2.   Use the mouse to highlight the individual drive icons.

3.   Specify the drive types you want to show by clicking on
the check boxes in Drive Types area. If you want to allow
access to the highlighted drives only, check the Allow Access to Selected Drives Only box. Select the Left or Right
Placement button.

4.   If you don't want the drive icons to show at all, clear the
Display Drive Icons check box.

5.   Select **OK** to confirm the choices or **Cancel** to return to the
previous configuration.

To Open a Drive Window

To open a Drive Window, double-click on the drive icon on the
desktop or select Window ➤ Open Drive Window. You can have
more than one Drive Window for the same drive open at the same
time, and windows for more than one drive can be open as well.
Figure II.2 illustrates the component parts of a Drive Window.

THE PARTS OF A DRIVE WINDOW

The various parts of the Drive Window work together to make it
easy to do most file operations with a click or two. The components
of the Drive Window are listed below.

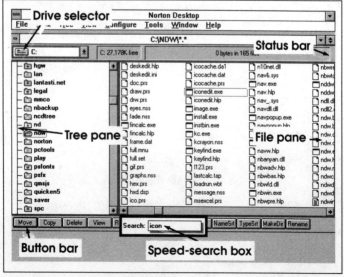

Figure II.2:   The parts of a Drive Window

The *status bar* displays information about the drive, directory, or file(s) selected.

The *drive selector* is a combination box. It allows you to change drives without opening up another Drive Window. To change drives, highlight this box and key in the letter of the drive or click on the drop-down box prompt button and select the drive.

The *button bar* has up to 14 buttons that can be configured to whatever file functions you most commonly use. To modify the default settings, see *Button Bar* earlier in this section. For the meaning of the default settings, select Configure ➤ Button Bar. In the Menu Item list, find and click on the item you want. A brief definition will pop up in the lower-left corner of the dialog box.

Panes make up the main body of the Drive Window. They display the selected drive's tree structure, a file list, and, with View Pane toggled on, the contents of the currently selected file. Select the panes you want open from the View menu.

The *speed-search box* is the quickest way to find a file or directory in either the Tree Pane or the File Pane. Note that you must start keying in characters for the speed-search box to appear. When you begin keying in the name of the file or directory, the speed-search box appears below the appropriate pane and the highlight bar moves to select the first file or directory that matches the keyed-in letters. When the highlight bar has moved to the file or directory you want, press **Enter** to select it.

If the Tree Pane is active, the speed-search box works in the Tree Pane. If the File Pane is active, the speed-search box works there. Press **Tab** to cycle the pane highlighter through the drive selector, Tree Pane, File Pane, and button bar.

To Refresh the Drive Windows

The display of files and directories in the Drive Windows does not always update automatically as moves, deletions, and so forth, are made. To update the display, select View ➤ Refresh, or press **F5**.

To Configure the Panes

From the View menu, select the following:

➤ Tree Pane to toggle the Tree Pane on and off.

➤ File Pane to toggle the File Pane on and off.

➤ View Pane to toggle the View Pane on and off.

➤ Show Entire Drive to replace the Tree and File Panes with a pane showing all the files on the drive and their locations.

To Filter the File Display in the File Pane

1. Select View ➤ Filter to bring up the Filter dialog box.

2. From the list in the File Type box, select the file types to display:

   All Files shows all the files. This is the default setting.

   Programs shows all executable programs (.COM, .EXE, .BAT, .PIF).

   Documents shows all document files (.DOC, .WRI, .TXT).

   Custom defines a custom filter.

3. If you chose Custom, fill in the combination box with the file specification(s) that you want displayed or choose from a list of recent selections. (Note that Custom can be used with wildcards in the file specifications.)

4. If you do not want subdirectories to be shown, clear the Show Directories check box.

5. From the Attributes box, choose which files to display by attribute.

6. If you want these setting to be in effect for future Drive Windows, click **Set Default**. Select **OK** to confirm the choices or **Cancel** to return to the previous configuration.

● EXAMPLES

- Toggle the **Hidden** attribute to blank to exclude hidden files.

- Toggle the **Archive** attribute to gray to see files regardless of whether they have been backed up or not.

- Choose **Custom**, then key in ~*.W?? to see all Lotus and Quattro Pro spreadsheet files.

- Choose **Custom**, then key in ~*.XLS *.W?? to see all spreadsheet files, including Excel files.

- **NOTE**   To change a file's attributes, see *Part Three, Attributes*.

To Change the File Pane Detail

1. Select View ➤ File Details to bring up the File Details dialog box.

2. Select the file details that you want to see displayed in the File Pane. Items marked with an X will show in the pane. The sample line shows how the files will appear.

3. If you want these settings to remain in effect for future operations, click on the **Set Default** button.

4. Select **OK** to confirm the choices, or **Cancel** to return to the previous configuration.

• OPTIONS

Icons toggles the display of file icons. An icon for a text file resembles a page with lines of writing on it. Executable files, such as programs and batch files, have icons that resemble on-screen windows. All other files have icons that look like a blank page of paper.

Date toggles the inclusion of file-creation date in the display.

Attributes toggles whether the file display includes the file attributes (Hidden, System, Read Only, or Archive).

Size toggles the inclusion of file size in the display.

Time toggles whether file-creation time is included in the display.

Directory toggles the display of the file's directory. (Active only in Show Entire Drive mode.)

To Change the Drive Window Font

1. Select View ➤ Font.

2. Select a font, font style, and size from the choices available. As you click on selections, a sample window shows you an example of the chosen combination.

3. You can also select the panes where you want the selected font to appear, as well as specify whether you want the new font selection to appear in all open Drive Windows.

4. Click **OK** to confirm your choices or **Cancel** to abandon changes.

To Change the Sort Order in the File Pane

1. Select View ➤ Sort By.

2. Use the mouse to highlight the file characteristic by which to sort or select ascending or descending sort order. The display will be updated immediately.

● **OPTIONS**

Name sorts alphabetically by file name.

Type sorts alphabetically by file extension.

Size sorts by file size.

Date sorts by file creation date and time.

Unsorted displays files in DOS order.

Ascending displays files in alphabetical order, smallest to largest, or most recent to oldest.

Descending displays files in reverse alphabetical order, largest to smallest, or oldest to most recent.

● **NOTES**   By default, the primary sort order is by file name. If type, size, or date is chosen as the primary sort, then the secondary sort is by name. The default sort is performed in ascending order (*A* before *Z* for file name, *1991* before *1992* for date, small before large for size) unless Descending Order is checked.

To Select and Deselect Files

1. To select files in a file pane, click on File ➤ Select. You can then choose All, Some, or Invert.

All will highlight every file shown in the File Pane.

Some will open a dialog box where you can type in the specifications for files you want to select using wildcard specifications. Or you can choose from a list of recent selections.

Invert will reverse the previous selection. That is, selected files will become unselected and unselected files will become selected.

2. To deselect files in a pane, choose File ➤ Deselect. The above three choices are also available with this command.

EDITOR

Any Editor program can be used to edit files in response to the File ➤ Edit command. When you installed Norton Desktop you had the option of selecting the Desktop Editor as your default editor. If you did not choose Desktop Editor, the default editor is Notepad.

To Set a New Default Editor

1. Select Configure ➤ Default Editor.

2. Key in the full path of the editor program that you want to use. If you don't know the exact name of the program, click on the **Browse** button. Highlight the name of the editor and then select **OK**. The editor's name will be returned to the Editor Program text box.

3. Then select **OK** again to save the new default editor.

LAUNCH MANAGER/LAUNCH LIST

The Launch Manager and Launch List are located in all the Control menus generated in Norton Desktop for Windows. Using Launch, you can open a file and its associated application from virtually anywhere in Norton Desktop for Windows. Files that are not part of the Launch List can also be started in quick fashion from a File Pane, Group Window, File Icon, or Command Line as described below.

To Add an Item to the Launch List

1. Select Launch Manager from any Control Box menu.

2. Click on **Add**. In the Text box, key in the name of the item as you want it to appear on the Launch List. If you want to be able to select the command by pressing a single letter, place an ampersand (&) just before that letter. On the Launch List the letter will be underlined.

3. In the Command Line box, key in the path for the item.

4. To associate a keyboard shortcut with the item, type in a two-key combination of Shift, Alt, or Ctrl and any second key. If you want the menu listing to show the shortcut key, click on the check box.

5. Click **OK** when you are finished.

● OPTIONS

- Type in the name of the Startup Directory if the application needs this information to run. You can see a list of directories by clicking on the **Directory** button.

- Select an option from the Run drop-down box if you want the launched file to run minimized or maximized. The default is normal.

- Check Prompt for Parameters if you want the launched item to pause to ask for needed information.

- Click on **Password** if you want to require a password to launch an item.

To Configure the Launch List

1. Select Launch Manager from any Control menu where it is available. Choose any of the following options to arrange the Launch List.

   Edit   Use the mouse to highlight a menu item and select Edit to modify any item on the menu.

   Delete   Highlight the item and then click on Delete to remove the item from the Launch List.

   Move Up/Move Down   Highlight a menu item and then click on Move Up or Move Down to change an item's position on the Launch List.

2. Click **OK** to confirm your choices.

To Launch a File from the Launch Manager

Pull down the Control menu anywhere in Norton Desktop for Windows. Highlight Launch List and a list of launchable programs and documents will drop down. Select the desired item and the application will execute.

To Launch a File from a File Pane

1. Select Window ➤ Open Drive Window or double-click on the appropriate drive icon.

2. Then double-click on the file name in the Drive Window or drag the file to a desktop application icon. A representation of a rocket will appear over the top of the icon and the file will launch.

To Launch a File from a Group Window

Double-click on the selected icon in its Group Window.

To Launch a File from a File Icon

1. Open the appropriate Drive Window and select the file from the file list.

2. Drag the file's icon to the name of the application on the list. This name must have an .EXE, .COM, .BAT, or .PIF extension. The application will execute and the file will open.

Note that before the application executes, a Warning message appears if you have selected Mouse Operations from the Configure Confirmation menu:

Are you sure you want to start *(application)* **using** *(file name)* **as the initial file?**

● **NOTE** This procedure can also be used to open files not associated with an application. In addition, it will work with a file that has an extension associated with a different application from the one you want to use. However, in Version 1.0, if you drag the file to an application icon on the desktop, the file will not open, and the file icon will remain on the desktop until you close it.

To Launch a File from the Command Line

1. Select File ➤ Run.

2. If the file is associated with an application, key in the file name and extension only. If the file is not associated with an application, key in the full pathname.

● **OPTIONS**

Startup Directory becomes the DOS default directory. If left blank, the default directory will be the one in which the launched program resides.

Run Style defines the look of the program when launched. Normal will cause applications to launch in their normal configuration. **Minimized** applications will shrink to icon size as soon as they are launched. **Maximized** files will appear full screen on your desktop.

Directory (*Browse* in Version 1.0) allows you to search through all drives and directories to select applications and files.

Prompt for Parameters (Version 2.0) when checked will prompt you for parameters when the program is launched.

Password (Version 2.0) lets you specify a password that will be required to launch the program.

Previous launches (Version 1.0 only) gives you a list of recent applications launched. Click on the prompt button next to the Run Window's Command Line text box.

See Also   *Associating a File Extension with a Program, Drive Windows*

MENUS

By default, the Norton Desktop menu bar shows short menus that contain only the most commonly used commands. Full menus can be installed by selecting Configure ➤ Full Menus. In the Load Menu dialog box, select Full Menus and click **OK**.

The menus and the menu bar are not fixed. You can add new menus and redesign existing menus in any way that suits you. If you specify a password, only users who know it will be able to get to the full and custom menus.

When you select Configure ➤ Edit Menus, you will see the Edit Menus dialog box, as shown in Figure II.3.

1.   Choose Configure ➤ Edit Menus.

2.   In the Available Commands box are all the standard menu commands. Scroll through the list and highlight the command you want. When you pick an item, a brief description of its function will appear in the lower-left corner of the dialog box.

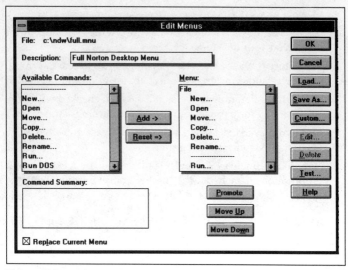

Figure II.3: The Edit Menus dialog box

3.   In the Menu List box, highlight the item that you want to directly follow the new function.

4.   Click on the **Add** button and the new command will be inserted right above the highlighted menu item. Click **OK**.

● **NOTE**   If you do not highlight a menu item, the Add function will not work.

To Delete a Menu Item

1.   Select Configure ➤ Edit Menus.

2.   Highlight the item you want to delete in the Menu box.

3.   Click on the **Delete** button. The item will be deleted. Click **OK** to exit the dialog box.

To Make a Custom Menu

1.   Select Configure ➤ Edit Menus.

2.   Click on the **Custom** button in the Edit Menus dialog box.

3. In the Type of Item box, click on the radio button for New Menu.

4. Key in the title for the menu in the text box. Click **OK** when you are finished.

5. To preview the results, click the **Test** button in the Edit Menus box to see what the new menu will look like. The title will appear as the leftmost menu in the menu bar. Use the Control menu to close the Test Custom Menus window.

6. Click **OK** when you are finished.

• **NOTE** To include an Alt-key accelerator in the menu name, key in an ampersand (&) directly in front of the accelerator letter. For example, key in *&Sales* and the menu will be highlighted when you enter the Alt-S key combination.

To Create a Library of Custom Menus

You can save one or more custom menus and have them available as you need them. These menus can be password-protected to limit access to them.

1. After you have created a menu in the Edit Menus dialog box, type in a new description in the Description text box. Click on the **Save As** button.

2. In the Save Menu As dialog box, a list of menu files will be in the Files box. In the File text box, type the name for the menu you want to save.

3. Click **OK** when you are finished.

• **NOTE** You can access the list of stored menus by selecting Configure ➤ Load Menu or by clicking on the **Load** button in the Edit Menus dialog box.

To Create a Custom Menu Item

1. Select Configure ➤ Edit Menus.

2. Click on the **Custom** button in the Edit Menus dialog box.

3. Under Type of Item, click on New Command.

4. In the text box, key in the name of the item as you want it to appear in the menu.

5. In the Command Line text box, key in the name of the program, script, or file that you want to launch when this menu item is selected. The command line must be either the complete path for the program to be launched or a file name with an associated extension.

6. If you want a shortcut key, enter the key or key combination in the Shortcut Key text box. Click on the check box if you want the shortcut key to display in the menu listing.

7. Click **OK**. Preview the menu by clicking on the **Test** button. Select **OK** again when you are finished.

To Edit a Menu Item

1. Select Configure ➤ Edit Menus.

2. Highlight the menu item you wish to edit and click on the **Edit** button to open the Edit Menu Item Text dialog box.

3. In the text box, key in the name as you want it to appear on the menu. Include an ampersand (&) directly in front of the letter that you want underlined.

4. Type in a shortcut key, if you want one, and click on the check box if you want the shortcut key to show in the menu.

5. The original setting for the item is shown at the top of the dialog box. Click on the **Original** button if you want to restore it. The **Original** option is not available if the item is one you created and not an original menu choice.

6. Select **OK** when you are finished or **Cancel** to abandon the operation.

To Change the Order of Menu Items

1. Open the Edit Menus dialog box by selecting Configure ➤ Edit Menus.

2. Using the scroll bar on the Menu box, highlight the item that you want to move.

- To move the item up one position, click on **Move Up**.
- To move the item down one position, click on the **Move Down** button.
- To promote an item up though the menu hierarchy, highlight it and click on the **Promote** button. To demote the item, click on the **Move Down** button.

3. Use the **Test** button to view the menu you have constructed. Then close the Test Custom Menu box and click **OK** when you are finished.

• **NOTE** Items can also be moved up and down by clicking on them and then dragging them to the position you want.

Names that are flush left in the Menu list are menu bar items. Indented under these are items directly under a menu title. The next indentation is for items in a cascaded menu.

To Remove a Menu or Menu Item

1. Select Configure ➤ Edit Menus.

2. In the Menu box, highlight the item you want to remove.

3. Click on the **Delete** button. The item will be deleted without further warning. If you choose a menu, a warning box will open advising you that the menu and all the items below it will be deleted if you proceed. Make your choice and click **OK** when the deletion is finished.

To Restore Original Menus

If you decide to either rebuild your custom menus or abandon them completely, you can easily reset the menu to its original configuration.

1. Select Configure ➤ Edit Menus.

2. Click on the **Reset** button. A warning will appear to inform you that you will be overwriting your custom choices. Click **Yes** if you want to proceed.

3. Click **OK** when you are finished.

PASSWORDS

If a password dialog box appears, it means that you have entered an area where a password is required. Passwords can be maintained in several areas:

- In custom menus, passwords can be set to prevent users from accessing certain menu commands. This type of password is set using the Configure ➤ Menu Password command.

- In a Launch List, a password can be required for an item to be launched.

- For Quick Access, passwords can restrict the use of groups or objects in Quick Access. (See *Part Four, Quick Access*.)

- With the Screen Saver, a password can be required to unlock the screen and keyboard when the Screen Saver is activated. (See *Part Four, Screen Saver*.)

To Set a Menu Password

1. Select Configure ➤ Menu Password.

2. Key in the password that you want in the **New Password** text box. The password, which can be up to 20 characters long, appears as asterisks (*) to ensure privacy.

3. Press **OK** and the **Confirm Password** box will become active. Key in the password a second time to confirm it and choose **OK** again.

Note that once a password has been set, you will need to enter it to use the **Load Menu** option.

● **NOTE**   To make the password permanent, you must choose
Configure ➤ Save Configuration or check the **Save Configuration
on Exit** check box in the Preferences dialog box (reached by choosing
Configure ➤ Preferences). Otherwise, the password will be in effect
for this session of Norton Desktop for Windows only.

To Remove a Menu Password

1. Select Configure ➤ Menu Password.

2. The Change Password dialog box will open with the Old
Password text box active. Key in the old password and
click **OK** or press **Enter**.

3. In the New Password text box, key in the new password
and click **OK**. If you want no password, press **Enter**.

4. The next box will ask you to confirm the password or to
confirm that want to delete the old password. Either key
in the new password and click **OK** or click **Yes** to confirm
that you want no password.

TREE VIEWER

The Tree menu allows you to select the degree of detail you want to
see in the Tree Pane portion of Drive Windows and Browse dialog
boxes. To use expandable and collapsible trees, click on the Use Collapsible Tree option on the Tree menu. This will make the expand
and collapse commands available. When this option is enabled, you
do not need to use the Refresh command (F5), because the tree information will be continually and automatically updated.

● **OPTIONS**

Expand One Level shows directories one level below the directory that is selected. Also available by pressing the plus (+) key
on the numeric keypad or by double-clicking on a file folder
that displays a plus sign.

Expand Branch shows all directories and subdirectories below the currently selected directory. Also enabled by pressing the asterisk key (*) on the numeric keypad.

Expand All shows all directories and subdirectories on the chosen drive. Also available by pressing Ctrl followed by the asterisk key (*) on the numeric keypad.

Collapse Branch hides all directories and subdirectories under the currently chosen directory. Can also be activated either by pressing the minus key (–) on the numeric keypad or by double-clicking on a folder that displays a minus sign.

SAVING THE CONFIGURATION

Changes in custom menus, shortcut keys, SmartErase, and Launch List will be saved automatically. Also, when you select a **Set Default** button in a dialog box, any changes you've made will be be preserved for future sessions. But you must use one of two save methods to make other changes permanent. The two methods have some overlapping functions, but they are not identical.

To Save the Appearance of Your Desktop

This method will preserve the appearance of your desktop as you leave it.

1. Select Configure ➤ Preferences.

2. Check the **Save Configuration on Exit** box.

3. Click **OK** when you are finished. When you next start Norton Desktop for Windows, the desktop will be as it was when you left it.

To Restart with a Standard Desktop

Arrange the desktop the way you want it to appear when you next start Norton Desktop for Windows. Choose Configure ➤ Save Configuration. Note that the desktop will continue to reopen with this appearance until the next time you choose Configure ➤ Save Configuration.

Part Three

Managing Files

ATTRIBUTES

Files can have one of four possible *attributes*—hidden, system, read-only, or archive. Usually, hidden files are not visible, but you can see them in Norton Desktop for Windows if desired. System files too are usually hidden from view. DOS uses the system attribute to designate files that it employs during its initial boot sequence.

Read-only files can be viewed with the Viewer or copied, but they cannot be edited, changed, or deleted. The archive attribute indicates whether a file has been backed up since the last time it was modified.

To Change File Attributes

1. Open a Drive Window.

2. Highlight the file you wish to change.

3. Select File ➤ Properties.

4. From the options in the Attributes box, select the attribute settings you want. If more than one file is selected, the option boxes have three states. Leave grey if you want to leave the attribute unchanged. Clear the box to remove an attribute for all selected files. Click twice to check the box and turn on an attribute for all selected files.

5. Select **OK** to confirm the operation or **Cancel** to abandon the change.

● EXAMPLE

If you want to make sure that a file is designated read-only, change the Read Only attribute box to an X. If you want to ensure that the file is not marked read-only, click on the Read-only attribute box until it is blank. If the file you have highlighted does not have a greyed read-only status (or other attribute), you cannot make it grey.

● **NOTE** If no file is highlighted, but a Group window is active, the Properties dialog box will open, as shown in Figure III.1. This dialog box allows you to modify group properties, including the group's icon startup directory, shortcut keys, and password.

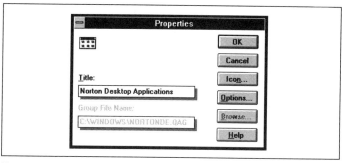

Figure III.1: The Properties dialog box

COPYING FILES

The Copy command lets you copy a single file or whole subdirectories. It can be used from the desktop or in Drive Windows. You activate the Copy command from the File drop-down menu, by pressing **F8**, or from the button bar (in Drive Windows). You can also click on file or subdirectory icons and drag them to their target locations.

To Copy a File or Files

1. Open a Drive Window.

2. Highlight the file or files that you want to copy. If you want to copy a subdirectory or subdirectories, highlight them.

3. Then use *one* of the following methods:

● Select File ➤ Copy.

- Press **F8**.
- Click the **Copy** button on the button bar.
- Drag the file to another open Drive Window, to the directory tree on the left side of the Drive Window, or to a drive icon.

4. If you drag and drop the file, you will be asked to confirm the copy operation. Otherwise, the Copy dialog box opens with a Destination combination box. Key in the destination, select from the list of recent destinations, or click on **Select** to open an enhanced Copy dialog box, and then choose the destination. This enhanced box also shows the amount of disk space used and the amount of free disk space remaining.

5. Select **OK** to begin the copy operation or **Cancel** to abandon it.

● **NOTES**   To copy subdirectories from the source directory, check the Include Subdirectories box in the Copy dialog box.

If you activate a group instead of a file, the Copy dialog box opens. To copy an object in one group window to another, click on the item while pressing **Ctrl**. Keep the **Ctrl** key depressed while dragging the icon to its destination. To copy a group window, drag the group icon into another group window.

DELETING FILES

The File ➤ Delete command allows you to delete a single file, multiple files, or entire subdirectories.

To Delete a File or Files

1. Open a Drive Window.
2. Highlight the file(s) or subdirectory you wish to delete.

3. Select File ➤ Delete, press the **Delete** button on the button bar, or press **Del** on your keyboard.

4. A Delete dialog box opens with the name of the selected file in a text box. Choose **OK** if you wish to delete the file. A warning window appears with these choices: Yes; Yes to All; No; Cancel. You must choose one. To remove this step, toggle off the Delete option in the Confirmation dialog box (choose Configure ➤ Confirmation).

● **SHORTCUT**   Click on the file or subdirectory in a Drive Window and drag it to the SmartErase or Shredder icon on the desktop.

● **NOTE**   If no group or Drive Window is open on the desktop, select Find ➤ Delete.

FIND AND SUPERFIND

When you select File ➤ Find, the SuperFind window opens. Super-Find can search for a specific file or for files that match a specific pattern, such as all files with the letters *MEMO* in their filenames, or all files with a .TXT extension. SuperFind can also perform a text search for files that contain text you are looking for.

Using the combination boxes and the **More** button, your search can be defined in a number of ways: according to the filename, extension, location on the drive, and even the time of day the file was created.

To Search for a File

1. Select File ➤ Find. Key in the name of the file including any extension in the Find Files box or click on the arrow next to the box to see default choices.

2. In the Where box, key in the path to be searched or select an option from the combination box.

3. Click on the **Find** button. The Directory line at the bottom of the dialog box shows the progress of the search. Files matching the criteria in the Find Files box will appear in a SuperFind Drive Window below the dialog box. Each subsequent search will produce a new Drive Window unless you toggle on Options ➤ Reuse Drive Window.

To Search for Text in a File

1. Key in the range of files and areas to be searched in the Find Files and Where boxes. If you want to search all files, click the prompt button on the Find Files combination box and select All Files.

2. In the With Text box, key in the text string that you want to find. The total amount of text, including spaces, must be no more than 30 characters. For an exact match, including upper- and lowercase letters, select Options ➤ Match Upper/Lowercase. Your four most recent text searches can be seen by clicking on the With Text prompt button.

3. When you have filled in all the search parameters, click the **Find** button.

● OPTIONS: FIND FILES BOX

All files is the same as the *.* file specification.

All files except programs searches for all files except those with .EXE, .COM, and .BAT extensions.

Database files searches for all dBASE-compatible files (.DB?) and all Q&A data files (.DTF)

Documents finds all .DOC, .TXT, and .WRI files.

Programs finds files with program extensions: .EXE, .COM, and .BAT.

Spreadsheet Files finds all Lotus (.WK?) and Excel (.XLS) worksheets.

● NOTES
You can use the standard DOS wildcards * and ? to specify files in the Find Files box, plus the pipe character (|), which represents one or zero characters.

Find and SuperFind   **43**

You can search for several types of files at once by separating each
file specification with a delimiter character: comma(,), semicolon(;),
plus sign (+), or a space.

To exclude a file type from your search, precede it with a minus
sign (–).

● EXAMPLES

¦ ¦ ¦.* searches for all filenames with three or fewer characters.

LET*.* searches for all filenames beginning with the characters
LET.

***.TXT,*.BMP** searches for .TXT and .BMP files.

***.* –.INI** searches for all files except those with the .INI
extension.

● OPTIONS: THE WHERE BOX

Current drive only

All drives

All drives except floppies

Current directory and subdirectories

Current directory only

Floppy drives only

Local hard drives only

Network drives only

Path

● OPTIONS: THE MORE BUTTON

This button opens up the SuperFind window, as shown in Figure III.2,
so you can define your choices even further. With these options you
can set the following:

Attributes are tri-state boxes and three-way toggles. A blank
check box means the program will search only for files with attribute bit turned off. An *X* in the box means files must have
this bit on. A grayed box means the setting of the bit is ignored.

44 Managing Files

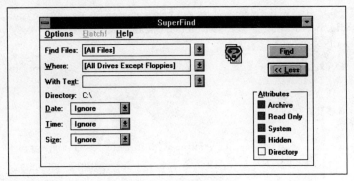

Figure III.2: The expanded SuperFind window

Date, Time, and Size boxes are set to Ignore by default. Click
on any of the prompt buttons to see the choices available. When
you select one of these options, one or more text boxes pop up for
you to complete.

To Set Up Search Sets

The default file and location search sets can be modified or deleted
and new sets can be added up to a total of 16 file sets and 16 location sets.

1. Select Options ➤ Search Sets to see the Search Sets win-
    dow, shown in Figure III.3.

2. Click on either the **File Sets** or **Location Sets** button.

3. To add a search set, click **Add**. Key in the name of the
    set and the definition in the text boxes. Wildcards and
    delimiters, as defined above, can be used. Click **OK** to
    confirm the addition. The new set will be added to the
    Search Sets list.

4. To edit or delete a set, highlight the set with the mouse
    and click on **Edit** or **Delete**. Click **OK** to confirm the
    change.

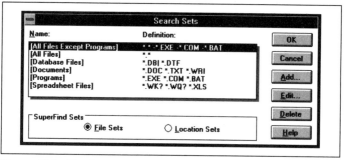

Figure III.3: The Search Sets window

● **WARNING**   Use the **Delete** button with caution. The deletion will be made immediately without a warning notice. If you press **Delete** in error, click on the **Cancel** button to save the deleted item.

To Create a Batch File from a File List

1.   After SuperFind has found your file or files, select Batch from the menu bar.

2.   Key in a name for the batch file in the Save As box. Select the **Browse** button to browse for a directory in which to place the batch file.

3.   Key in any batch instructions you want in the Insert Before Filename and Append After Filename text boxes. Select options that you want to include. Choose **Launch** to test the batch file in DOS. An error in the batch file will cause it to abort. To find the source of the error, toggle on PAUSE After Each Command to step through the batch.

4.   Select **OK** to save the batch file.

● **OPTIONS: BATCH FILES**

Full Path inserts the full path name for each file in the batch file if files in the batch file are located in different directories.

Spaces Around Filename automatically enters blank spaces
before and after the filename on each command line of the
batch file. The default is On.

CALL Each Command inserts the batch language CALL command at the beginning of each line of the batch file.

PAUSE After Each Command inserts a pause after each operation in the batch file. When launching a batch file you can then
examine each command as it is executed.

See Also   *Part Five, Batch Language*

● **OPTIONS MENU**

OEM Text instructs SuperFind to use the OEM character set
instead of the ANSI character set. Toggle this on when you are
searching files made with a DOS text editor.

Animation turns the animated search icon on and off. The
search should be faster with Animation turned off.

Running Man substitutes the running man figure for the
SuperFind icon. He won't actually run unless Animation is
toggled on.

Unless **Reuse Drive Window** is toggled on, each search will
generate its own Drive Window.

Exclusive Search stops all other programs and prevents task-
switching while the search is being performed. For faster searches, toggle this option on. To have searches performed in the
background while you do other work, toggle this option off.

Minimized Search minimizes the window to an icon while
conducting the search.

MAKING DIRECTORIES

When directories become too large, you can make a new subdirectory to keep track of your files.

To Make a New Directory

1. Choose File ➤ Make Directory.

2. A dialog box opens and you can key in the name, including the path, of the directory you wish to create in the New Directory text box. Click on **Select** to see a directory tree of the current drive. Other drives can be selected in the Destination drop-down box.

3. Select the **OK** button to confirm your choice.

MOVING FILES

To move a file rather than copy it, follow the steps below.

To Move a File

1. Open a Drive Window.

2. Highlight the file(s) or subdirectory you wish to move.

3. Select File ➤ Move, click the **Move** button on the button bar, or press **F7**. In the To text box, key in the file destination, including the path.

4. Click **OK** when you're finished.

● **NOTES** To choose a destination, click on the **Select** button to see a directory tree of the current drive, including a display of available space. Click on the directory name of the target location, and then click **OK**. Other drives can be selected from the Destination drop-down box.

If a group is highlighted instead of a file or subdirectory, the Move Group dialog box is opened.

OPENING FILES

When you select File ➤ Open, one of the following things happens, depending on what you have highlighted:

- The selected file is launched (files and applications).
- The highlighted item in the active group window is opened (subdirectories).

If nothing is active, the Open option is dimmed.

PRINTING

To Print a File

1. Select File ➤ Print.

2. Key in the name of the file to be printed in the Print text box.

3. Select **OK**.

Click on the Browse button to see a list of files sorted by directory within the current drive. Use the mouse to change drives and directories and to select a filename.

● **SHORTCUT**   Drag the file's icon from an open Drive Window to the Printer Icon on the desktop.

● **NOTES**   If you drag the file to the Printer icon on the desktop, Norton Desktop for Windows checks to see if the file has an extension associated with an application in the associations list. If no association exists, Norton Desktop for Windows will ask if you want to print the file as text. If you select Yes, the file will be printed through the Desktop Editor.

If an association exists, the application will open and the name of the document file will be passed to the application. Norton Desktop for Windows will then send the keystrokes *Alt-F P* to the application. This assumes that the application has the menu command File ▶ Print. Norton Desktop for Windows then minimizes the application and switches back to the desktop. If these steps do not work—and they won't for many non-Windows applications—you will need to follow the steps in the section *To Set Up a Print Keystroke Sequence*.

VERSION 1.0: If the file has no association, Norton Desktop for Windows will ask if you want the file printed unformatted. If you select Yes, the file will print. The results, however, may be incomplete or garbled.

To Set Up a Print Keystroke Sequence

1. Using a text editor, open the existing NDW.INI file.

2. Add a line with the heading

(Print Start)

3. Under the heading, add a line in the form

filename.exe=start key sequence

where *filename* is the name of the program and *start key sequence* describes the keystrokes that will print the current file.

4. Next, add a line with the heading called

(Print Stop)

5. Under that, add a line in the form

filename.exe=stop key sequence

where *filename* is the name of the program and *stop key sequence* describes the keystrokes that will close and exit the application.

6. Save the changes to NDW.INI and restart Norton Desktop for Windows.

The start and stop key sequence can contain **Alt** and **Ctrl** keys as well as function keys using the following codes:

Key	Code
Alt-key	!key
Ctrl-key	^key
Enter	{Enter} or ~
F1–F16	{F1} through {F16}

To Print Associated Files Directly

1. Using a text editor, open the file NDW.INI. Add a line with the heading named

   (Print Start)

2. In that section, add the line

   filename.exe=

   where *filename* is the name of the program associated with the file you want to print. Leave the right side of the equal sign blank.

3. Save the changes to NDW.INI and restart Norton Desktop for Windows.

To Change Printers or Printer Settings

1. Select File ➤ Print. To change the printer, open the drop-down box and select another printer. Select Setup to check or change settings.

2. The Setup options are the same as the Windows printer settings. Changes made here affect how the printer works with all Windows applications.

RENAMING FILES

A single file or a subdirectory can be renamed quickly. Simply enter
the name or search for it as described below.

To Rename a File or Subdirectory

1. Open a Drive Window.
2. Highlight the file or subdirectory you want to rename.
3. Select File ➤ Rename.
4. Key in the new path and name in the To text box.
5. Select **OK**.

● **NOTE**   For help in finding the file to be renamed, select the
Browse button for a drive and directory tree. Double-click on your
choice or highlight it and click **OK**.

RUNNING PROGRAMS

If you don't use a program or document often enough to have it as
an item in a group window, use **Run** to launch it when needed.

To Use Run

1. Select File ➤ Run.
2. In the Command Line text box, type the full name including the path of the program or file you want to launch. A
   document must have an association to the program that
   runs it. You can also click on the prompt button for a list
   of recently launched files.

3. Select an option from the Run Style box.

4. Click **OK** to confirm your choices.

● OPTIONS: RUN STYLE

Normal runs in an intermediate size window.

Minimized immediately shrinks the program to an icon on the desktop after opening.

Maximized opens a window filling the screen.

RUNNING DOS

Select File ➤ Run DOS to temporarily exit Windows to the DOS prompt. Type **Exit** to return to Windows.

VIEWER

Viewer displays a file according to its extension. For example, .DOC indicates a file written in Microsoft Word. If the file lacks an extension, Viewer will display the file according to the default setting. If you have a TIFF graphics image file, for example, without an extension or with an extension that does not identify it as a TIFF file, you will not be able to view the file unless the Viewer's default setting is TIFF (Grayscale and Color).

To View a File

1. Double-click on the Viewer desktop icon or the File Viewer icon in the Norton Desktop group window.

2. Select File ➤ Open. Choose the file you want to view from the Browse box. Click **OK**. The file will appear in its own window inside the Viewer window.

● **SHORTCUT**   Click on the file in an open Drive Window and drag it to the Viewer desktop icon.

● **OPTIONS: FILE MENU**

Open opens a Browse window from which you can select a file to view.

Close closes the file in the active window.

Exit closes the File Viewer window.

● **OPTIONS: VIEWER MENU**

Font (**VERSION 2.0** only) opens the Windows font selection dialog box. Select a typeface, style, and size. An example of your selection will appear in the Sample box. Click **OK** and the entire file in the Viewer will appear in the new font.

OEM Text (**VERSION 2.0** only) shows the file in the Viewer window using the OEM character set instead of the ANSI character set.

Set Current Viewer changes the file translation for the active window. For example, if you have a text file in the active window, select Hex Dump to see the file in a hexadecimal translation.

Set Default Viewer changes the translator for the next file you select to view. If the file has an extension recognized as the default by Norton Desktop, it will be opened in the recognized format. If not, the program will attempt to open the file in the translation specified here.

● OPTIONS: SEARCH MENU

Find searches for a text string or data that you specify. Key in the characters you want to search for and click **OK**. The program will search the active window for that string and stop when finds it.

Find Next searches for the next occurrence of the string specified.

Find Previous searches backward in the active window for the previous occurrence of the specified string.

GoTo brings up the GoTo dialog box when you are viewing a spreadsheet or database, to let you input a specific row and column or field and record for the program to find.

● OPTIONS: WINDOW MENU

Cascade arranges the open file windows in stair-steps with the title bars showing and the active file on top.

Tile arranges the open windows so all are visible. The amount of space allotted to each window diminishes as the number of open files increases.

Close All closes all the open file windows but leaves the Viewer window open.

Hide All: Causes all windows to disappear from the desktop. To reopen, pull down menu and click UnHide.

Arrange Desktop: Rearranges desktop icons to their original positions.

Arrange Group Icons: Reorders group icons inside windows.

View Group As: Sets the group view format.

● NOTE   At the bottom of this menu is a list of open files with a check mark designating the active window. If you have more than nine files open, click on **More Windows** to see a complete list. You can click on a file's name to make it active.

Part Four

Tools and Utilities

BATCH BUILDER

You use the Batch Builder program to edit batch files with the extension .WBT. All the commands in Batch Builder are duplicates of those in the Desktop Editor, with the exception of the Tools menu.

● OPTIONS: TOOLS MENU

Test runs the commands in the current document as a batch file. Use this command to ensure a batch will run correctly.

Reference opens the batch language Reference dialog box where you can look up any of 150 commands.

Macro Builder opens the Macro Builder dialog box. See *Macro Builder* below for more information on building macros.

To Create a Batch File

1. Open Batch Builder either by selecting Tools ➤ Batch Builder or double-clicking on the Batch Builder icon in the Norton Desktop group window.

2. Select File ➤ New and key in the commands for the batch file.

3. Select File ➤ Save or File ➤ Save As. The Save File dialog box will open. Key in a name for the file, including the .WBT extension. Then click **OK** or press **Enter** to save the file.

● EXAMPLE

To create a batch file to open WordPerfect 5.1 and load a file called DAILY.LOG where you keep your work notes, open the Batch Builder, and key in the following line:

    Run("WP.PIF","DAILY.LOG")

Then select File ➤ Save or File ➤ Save As and key in a name for the batch file, for example, *DAILYLOG.WBT*. Select **OK** to save the file.

Now, open a Drive Window and drag the file DAILYLOG.WBT onto the desktop. Then, whenever you want to open your log, just double-click on the icon.

To Edit an Existing Batch File

1. Open Batch Builder either by selecting Tools ➤ Batch Builder or double-clicking on the Batch Builder icon in the Norton Desktop group window.

2. Select File ➤ Open and then select the file to edit by highlighting the filename and selecting **OK** or by double-clicking on the file name.

3. Edit the batch file.

4. Select File ➤ Save .

● EXAMPLE

To make the batch file that opens our daily log file a bit more intelligent, let's edit it. Open Batch Builder and then open the file DAILYLOG.WBT. Edit it so that it reads

If WinExist("WordPerfect") == @TRUE Then Goto ACTIVATE

Run("WP.PIF","DAILY.LOG")

Goto END

:ACTIVATE

WinActivate("WordPerfect")

:END

Then select File ➤ Save. Now when you double-click on the DAILYLOG.WBT icon, which should be on the desktop, the batch file will check to see whether you are already running a copy of WordPerfect; if you are, the batch file will simply switch to it instead of trying to open it again, which would result in an error message.

To Insert a Batch Command
into the Current Batch File

1. Select Tools ➤ Reference (Version 1.0: **Reference!** menu).

2. Scroll through the alphabetical list of commands in the Command scroll box.

3. Highlight the command that you want to insert into the batch file. A description of the command including its syntax and an example will appear in the Description box.

4. Double-click on the command or select **Add** to add the command at the current cursor position

5. Select **Close** to close the Reference window.

● **NOTE**   Fewer options are available for Batch Builder in Version 1.0, but the functions that have been carried forward into Version 2.0 are identical for both versions. See *Desktop Editor* for information on specific options.

CALCULATORS

Three calculators are included with Norton Desktop for Windows. (Version 1.0 has only two, the ten-key and the scientific.) The *ten-key* calculator is useful for simple calculations and for keeping running totals. It also includes a tape function. The *scientific* calculator can do simple arithmetic calculations, as well as more advanced functions such as logarithms, factorials, and exponents. The *financial* calculator, new to Version 2.0, calculates interest, amortization, bond yields, and other simple financial calculations.

USING THE FINANCIAL CALCULATOR

The financial calculator is a sophisticated accessory with 100 registers of storage, a full set of financial functions, and a helpful set of dialog boxes to simplify common financial calculations. Like the scientific calculator, it uses the Reverse Polish Notation (RPN)

method and stacks to handle more complicated calculations. For information on RPN and the mechanics of how to use the financial calculator, see the corresponding sections below under the *scientific calculator*. To perform calculations on amortization, bond yields and prices, dates and times, depreciation, discounted cash flow, simple interest, and statistics, pull down the Compute menu, shown in Figure IV.1.

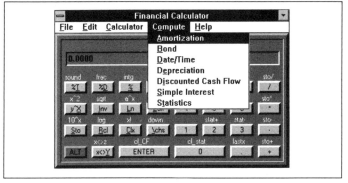

Figure IV.1: The Compute menu provides easy access to common financial calculations.

To Calculate Amortization

The Amortization dialog box provides an easy way to calculate the amortization of a loan, as well as its annual percentage rate.

1. Select Compute ➤ Amortization.

2. The Amortization dialog box opens, as shown in Figure IV.2.

3. Specify whether the function should solve for the principal, the periodic payment, or the interest rate.

4. Key in the number of payments on the loan.

5. If you are not solving for the principal amount, key the amount of the loan into the Principal Amount box.

6. If you know and are consequently not solving for the interest rate, key it into the Interest Rate box.

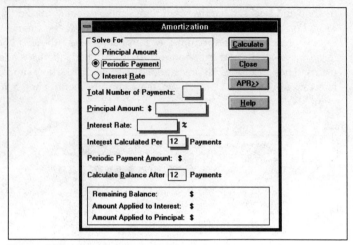

Figure IV.2: The Amortization dialog box

7. Key in the number of payments per interest period. (For annual interest rates and monthly payments, this number is 12.)

8. If you know and are consequently not solving for the amount of each payment, key it into the Periodic Payment Amount box.

9. Key in the number of payments the calculation is for.

10. Click on the **Calculate** button, and the value you were solving for, along with the remaining balance of the loan, the amount applied to interest and the amount applied to principal will be calculated and displayed.

11. To calculate the annual percentage rate (APR) of the loan, click on the **APR>>** button and key in the points and loan fees paid. Click on the **Calculate** button again, and the APR will be calculated and displayed.

To Calculate the Yield or Price of a Bond

The **Calculate Bond** dialog box provides a quick and easy way to calculate the yield of a bond or the price you should pay to realize the yield you desire.

1. Select Compute ➤ Bond.

2. The Calculate Bond dialog box opens.

3. Specify whether the function should solve for the bond's price or yield.

4. Select the date format to use.

5. Key in the quoted interest rate (coupon rate) for the bond.

6. Key in the settlement and maturity rates, using the date format you selected.

7. If you are calculating the bond's price, key your expected yield into the Yield to Maturity box and click on **Calculate**. The price you would need to pay to achieve the desired yield is calculated and displayed, along with accrued interest.

8. If you are calculating the bond's yield, key in the price for the bond and click on the **Calculate** button. The rate that the bond will yield if held to its maturity is calculated and displayed.

To Calculate the Difference between Two Dates or Times

The Date/Time dialog box provides a simple way to calculate the number of days between two dates or the number of hours and minutes between two times.

1. Select Compute ➤ Date/Time.

2. Select the beginning date and time and the ending date and time.

3. Click **Calculate** and the difference between the two times is calculated and displayed.

• OPTIONS

Click on the **Options** button to open the Date/Time Options dialog box.

> **Time Format** lets you choose between 12-hour format or 24-hour format.
>
> **Basis** lets you choose between a standard calendar month or the financial 30-day month.

To Calculate Depreciation

The Calculate Depreciation dialog box provides an easy way to calculate the depreciation of capital assets, allowing you to choose from three common methods of calculating depreciation.

1. Select Compute ➤ Depreciation.

2. The Calculate Depreciation dialog box opens.

3. Key in the cost of the asset, its salvage value, and expected life.

4. Choose the method of depreciation by clicking on the **Method** button. There are three choices:

   > **Straight-line** depreciates the same amount each year and is just the original cost, less the salvage value divided by the expected life.
   >
   > **Sum-of-Years-Digits** is an accelerated method that calculates depreciation much faster at the beginning of the asset's life than at its end.
   >
   > **Declining Balance**, another accelerated method of depreciating, calculates depreciation faster at the beginning than at the end. Choose between straight-line and absolute methods of declining-balance depreciation and enter the factor to use.

5. Key in the number of years of service to calculate the asset's depreciation for.

6. Click on the **Calculate** button, and the depreciated value and accumulated depreciation are figured and displayed.

To Calculate the Discounted Cash Flow

The Discounted Cash Flow dialog box provides a simple method of calculating either the net present value or internal rate of return.

1. Click on the **ALT** button and then the **cl_CF** key (the **ENTER** key) to clear the cash flow registers.

2. Key in the amount of the initial investment. Click on the **ALT** button and then the **CFj+** key (the *5* key). The value **1** appears in the display, which shows the number of entries in the cash-flow register.

3. Key in the rest of cash-flow entries, pressing the **CFj+** key after each entry. The display is updated each time to show the number of entries in the cash-flow register.

4. When you have entered all the cash-flow items, select Compute ➤ Discounted Cash Flow.

5. Enter the interest rate desired.

6. Click **Calculate** to calculate and display the net present value.

7. Check the Internal Rate of Return check box to calculate the internal rate of return.

To Calculate Simple Interest

The Simple Interest dialog box provides an easy way to calculate the simple interest return on an investment or cost of a loan.

1. Select Compute ➤ Simple Interest.

2. Key in the number of days of the loan or investment.

3. Key in the annual interest rate.

4. Key in the amount of the loan or investment.

5. Specify whether the function should compute based on the normal 365 day year or the financial 360 day year.

6. Click **Compute** and the accrued interest and combined value of interest and principal are calculated and displayed.

To Calculate Statistics

The Statistics dialog box provides an easy way to calculate a number of useful two-variable statistics values, including standard deviation, average, and weighted average.

1. Click on the **ALT** key and then the **cl_stat** key (the *0* key) to clear the statistical register.

2. Key in the first *y* value and click on the **ENTER** key, then key in the first *x* value and click on the **ALT** key followed by the **stat+** key (the *2* key). The value **1** appears in the display, indicating that there is one entry in the statistical register.

3. Key in the rest of the *x* and *y* values as described in step 2 above, using the **stat+** key to add them to the register. The number of entries in the register is displayed each time you click **stat+**.

4. Select Compute ➤ Statistics.

5. The average, standard deviation, and weighted average are displayed. To see the sum, sum of the squares, and sum of the product, click on the **More>>** button.

6. To estimate the next *x* or *y* value in a series, click on the **Estimate** button.

7. The Linear Estimation dialog box opens. Key in either the *x* or *y* value and click on the **Calculate** button. The estimated value for the other will be calculated and displayed.

Functions

The financial calculator has approximately 35 different mathematical and financial functions, depending on how you count them. Each can be accessed with the keyboard or mouse. A complete list of the functions and keystrokes is given in Table IV.1.

Table IV. 1: Financial Calculator Functions

Button	Keyboard	Function
	Ctrl-Ins	Copies display (*x* register) to Clipboard
	Shift-Ins	Pastes Clipboard contents to display (*x* register)
ALT	Alt	Enables Alt-mode functions
	F1	Help
%	%	Calculates *x* percentage of *y* register
%D	D	Calculates percent difference between *x* and *y* registers
%T	T	Calculates what percent *x* register is of the *y* register
+	+	Adds *y* register to *x* register
−	−	Subtracts *x* register from *y* register
×	*	Multiplies *y* register by *x* register
÷	/	Divides *y* register by *x* register
←	Backspace	Deletes last digit in display
ENTER	↵	Pushes value in display into *y* register, *y* register into *z* register, *z* register into *t* register, and deletes *t* register
\chs	\	Changes sign of display (*x* register)
10^x	Alt,S	Calculates 10 to the *x*th power
CFj+	Alt,5	Inserts value in *x* into cash flow register

Table IV.1: Financial Calculator Functions (continued)

Button	Keyboard	Function
CFj–	Alt,6	Removes value in x from cash flow register, if found
Clx	C	Clears the x register and the display
cl_CF	Alt,ENTER	Clears the cash flow register
cl_stat	Alt,0	Clears the statistics register
Down	Alt,\	Scroll stack downward
Eex	E	Inputs exponent of 10 (scientific notation)
e^x	Alt,L	Computes the natural exponent of x register
fix	Alt,8	Display in fixed decimal notation
frac	Alt,D	Fractional portion of x register.
intg	Alt,%	Integer portion of x register (truncates x)
Inv	I	Calculates the inverse of x register ($1/x$)
lastx	Alt,.	Replaces x register with previous value of x register
log	Alt,R	Returns the common logarithm of x register
Ln	L	Returns the natural logarithm of x register
mod	Alt,9	Returns the modulus of x/y (the remainder)
Rcl	R	Recalls contents of register 00–99 to register x
round	Alt,T	Rounds the x register to nearest whole number

Table IV.1: Financial Calculator Functions (continued)

Button	Keyboard	Function
sci	Alt,7	Selects display in scientific notation
sqrt	Alt,I	Calculates square root of x register
Sto	S	Stores contents of x register in register 00–99
sto+	Alt,plus	Adds contents of x register to contents of register nn and stores in register nn
sto−	Alt,minus	Subtracts contents of x register from contents of register nn and stores in register nn
sto×	Alt,*	Multiplies contents of x register by contents of register nn and stores in register nn
sto÷	Alt,/	Divides contents of register nn by contents of x register and stores in register nn
up	Alt,E	Scrolls stack upwards
x!	Alt,C	Returns the factorial of x register to the x register
x<>Y	Y	Swaps contents of x register and y register
x<>z	Alt,Y	Swaps contents of x register and z register
x^2	Alt,X	Squares value of x register
y^X	X	Raises x register to power of y register

USING THE SCIENTIFIC CALCULATOR

The scientific calculator is a sophisticated calculator with 100 registers of storage, a full set of trigonometric and scientific functions, and the ability to work with hex and octal numbers. It uses the Reverse Polish Notation method and stacks to handle more complicated calculations.

Reverse Polish Notation and Stacks

Conventional arithmetic places the operators between the operands, which works fine for simple calculations, but breaks down with more complex ones. The scientific calculator uses a four-element stack to handle "parentheses" formulas. A stack is a *Last In First Out* memory function. Reverse Polish Notation (RPN) when used with a stack, provides a simple but elegant solution. With RPN, you enter the operands, then the operator.

• EXAMPLES

$17 + 25 - 4 = 38$

Keystroke	Display
17	17
ENTER	17
25	25
+	42
4	4
−	38

$35 \div (3 + 2) = 7$

Keystroke	Display
35	35
ENTER	35
3	3

Keystroke	Display
ENTER	3
2	2
+	5
/	7

The Mechanics of the Scientific Calculator

You can use the mouse, the keyboard, or a combination of the two keys or functions on the calculator. To use the mouse, simply click on the desired button. To access the functions above each button, click on the **ALT** button. At the top of the calculator you'll see the *ALT* legend, as shown in Figure IV.3. Then press the button below the function you want. To use the keyboard, use the numbers and functions on the numeric keypad for number entry. For other functions, the key to use is capitalized and underlined in the display. For example, the cosine function is the *C* key. To access the functions above each button, click the **ALT** button first, then press the capitalized letter.

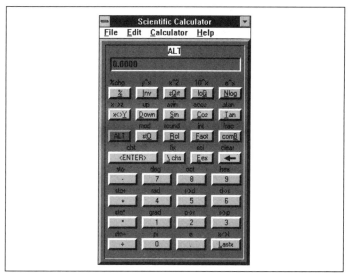

Figure IV.3: The ALT key provides access to the functions above the buttons.

To Display a Fixed Number of Decimal Places

The display can be set to a fixed number of decimal places. To set to three decimal places follow these steps:

1. Click on the **ALT** button first.
2. Click on the **\chs** button, which is underneath **fix**.
3. Click on the 3 button.

To Display Numbers in Scientific Notation

The display can also be set to scientific notation, with a fixed number of decimal places. To specify scientific notation with two decimal places:

1. Click on the **ALT** button.
2. Click on the button below **sci**, the **Eex** button.
3. Click on the 2 button.

To Display the Hex or Octal Equivalent

The hexadecimal or octal equivalent of the current integer value can be displayed. Note, however, that only the integer portion is displayed. The decimal portion is truncated.

1. Click on the **ALT** button.
2. Click on the button below **hex**, the **9** button. The hex equivalent of the integer portion is displayed. For octal, click on the button below **oct**, the **8** button.
3. To return to the previous display, click on the **ALT** button again, then click on the Backspace key.

• EXAMPLE

Key in the number **16** and press **Enter** or click on the **ENTER** button. The display shows

16.0000

Tap the **Alt** key or click on the **ALT** button, then press the **9** key or click on the button below **hex**. The display shows

10

which is 16 in hexadecimal notation. Tap the **Alt** key again and press the **8** key or click on the button below **oct**. The display changes to

20

which is the octal equivalent of 10 hex or 16 decimal.

Functions

The scientific calculator has approximately 50 mathematical and trigonometric functions, depending on how you count them. Each can be accessed with the keyboard or mouse. A complete list of the functions and keystrokes is given in Table IV.2.

Table IV.2: Scientific Calculator Functions

Button	Keyboard	Function
	Ctrl-Ins	Copies display (x register) to clipboard
	Shift-Ins	Pastes clipboard to display (x register)
ALT	Alt	Enables Alt-mode functions
	F1	Help
%	%	Calculates x percentage of y register
%chg	Alt,%	Calculates percent difference between x and y registers
+	+	Adds y register to x register
−	−	Subtracts x register from y register
×	*	Multiplies y register by x register

Table IV.2: Scientific Calculator Functions (continued)

Button	Keyboard	Function
÷	/	Divides y register by x register
←	Backspace	Deletes last digit in display
ENTER	↵	Pushes value in display into y register, y register into z register, z register into t register, deletes t register
\ chs	\	Changes sign of display (x register)
10^x	Alt,G	Calculates 10 to the xth power
acos	Alt,C	Calculates arc cosine of x register
asin	Alt,S	Calculates the arc sine of x register
atan	Alt,T	Calculates the arc tangent of x register
clear	Alt,Backspace	Clears x register, or clears hex/octal display
clst	Alt,↵	Clears stack (x, y, z, and t registers)
comB	B	Calculates the combinations of y register, x register at a time
Cos	C	Calculates the cosine of x register
d–>r	Alt,6	Converts x register from degrees to radians
deg	Alt,7	Display angles as degrees
Down	D	Scroll stack downward
e	Alt,.	x = Euler's constant (2.718…)

Table IV.2: Scientific Calculator Functions (continued)

Button	Keyboard	Function
Eex	E	Inputs exponent of 10 (scientific notation)
e^x	Alt,N	Computes the natural exponent of x register
Fact	F	Calculates the factorial of the x register ($x!$)
fix	Alt,\	Display in fixed decimal notation
frac	Alt,B	Fractional portion of x register.
grad	Alt,1	Use gradients
hex	Alt,9	Display integer portion of x register in hexidecimal (base 16)
int	Alt,F	Integer portion of x register (truncates x)
Inv	I	Calculates the inverse of x register ($1/x$)
Lastx	L	Replaces x register with previous value of x register
loG	G	Calculates the logarithm of x register
mod	Alt,O	Returns the modulus of x/y (the remainder)
Nlog	N	Calculates the natural logarithm of x register
oct	Alt,8	Displays integer portion of x register in octal (base 8)
p–>r	Alt,2	Converts x register, y register from polar to rectangular coordinates

---

Table IV.2: Scientific Calculator Functions (continued)

Button	Keyboard	Function
pi	Alt,0	x = pi (3.14159…)
r–>d	Alt,5	Converts x register from radians to degrees
r–>p	Alt,3	Converts x register, y register from rectangular coordinates to polar coordinates
rad	Alt,4	Changes display from degrees to radians
Rcl	R	Recalls contents of register 00–99 to register x
round	Alt,R	Rounds the x register to nearest whole number
sci	Alt,E	Selects display in scientific notation
Sin	S	Computes sine of x register
sQrt	Q	Calculates square root of x register
stO	O	Stores contents of x register in register 00–99
sto+	Alt,plus	Adds contents of x register to contents of register nn and stores in register nn
sto–	Alt,minus	Subtracts contents of x register from contents of register nn and stores inregister nn
sto×	Alt,*	Multiplies contents of x register by contents of register nn and stores in register nn

Table IV.2: Scientific Calculator Functions (continued)

Button	Keyboard	Function
sto÷	Alt,/	Divides contents of register *nn* by contents of *x* register and stores in register *nn*
Tan	T	Calculates the tangent of *x* register
up	Alt,D	Scrolls stack upwards
x<>t	Alt,L	Swaps contents of *x* register and *t* register
x<>Y	Y	Swaps contents of *x* register and *y* register
x<>z	Alt,Y	Swaps contents of *x* register and *z* register
x^2	Alt,Q	Squares value of *x* register
y^x	Alt,I	Raises *x* register to power of *y* register

USING THE TEN-KEY CALCULATOR

After opening the ten-key calculator, you can click on the minimize button to iconize it. Then the calculator will be immediately available on your desktop.

To Open the Ten-Key Calculator

1. Choose Tools ➤ Calculator or double-click on the Tape Calculator icon in the Norton Desktop window.

2. The last calculator you used will open. To switch between the financial, ten-key, and scientific calculators, click on the calculator menu. If one of the other calculators is open, select **Tape.**

3.   The ten-key calculator can be operated from the keyboard or by using mouse clicks. Table IV.3 lists each calculator key, the keyboard strokes necessary to access it, and its function.

Table IV.3: Keyboard Functions on the Ten-Key Calculator

Key	Keyboard	Function
AC	Ctrl-A	Clears all memory and keyboard registers
TAX	Ctrl-X	Calculates tax
GPM	Ctrl-G	Calculates gross profit margin
TXT	Shift-"	Turns text entry on and off
+/−	\	Changes sign
÷	/	Divides by the next entry
×	*	Multiplies by next entry
=	=	Equal
CE	Ctrl-E	Clears entry in the single-line display
C	Ctrl-C	Clear
−	−	Subtract
+	+	Add
%	%	Calculates percent
S	Shift-Enter	Subtotal
T	↵	Totals
MT	Ctrl-T	Totals and clears memory register
MS	Ctrl-S	Subtotals memory register
M−	Ctrl-minus	Subtracts current entry from memory. From the keyboard M− is Ctrl-minus.
M+	Ctrl-plus	Adds current entry to memory. From the keyboard M+ is Ctrl-plus.

To Change the Default Settings

1. Select File ➤ Setup. The Setup dialog box opens, as shown in Figure IV.4.

2. Make your selections.

3. Click **OK** when you're finished.

● SETUP OPTIONS

Notation is the setting for decimal places. The default setting is two decimal places.

Tax Rate is the sales tax percentage added to your total when you select the **TAX** key. Key in the tax rate you want to use.

Show Date and Time, if toggled on, puts the current date and time on each calculation.

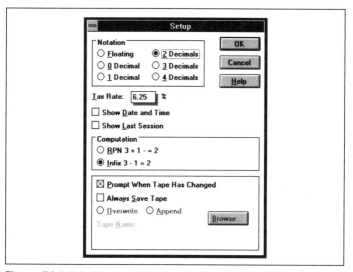

Figure IV.4: The Setup dialog box for the ten-key calculator

Show Last Session, if toggled on, displays the contents of your last work session when you start the calculator.

Computation allows you to select between RPN (Reverse Polish Notation, described in the *Scientific Calculator* section) and Infix. The default setting is Infix.

Prompt When Tape Has Changed opens a dialog box to ask if you want to save the changed tape before exiting the calculator.

Always Save Tape causes the tape to be saved automatically. You can choose to Overwrite a saved tape or Append the contents of this tape to a saved tape. The default name for the tape is in the Tape Name text box or you can type in another choice.

To Clear Your Data

- To clear a single display line, use the **Backspace** key or click on **CE**.

- To clear the memory register only, click on the **MT** key.

- To clear all transactions since your last total, click on **C**.

- To clear all registers and the tape, click on **AC**.

To Copy a Figure from the Calculator to a Windows Document

1. From the calculator's display, highlight the total to be copied.

2. Choose Edit ➤ Copy.

3. Select the target Windows document. Position the cursor where you want the answer placed.

4. Choose Edit ➤ Paste.

To Copy a Figure from a Windows Document to the Calculator

1. In the Windows document, select the numbers you want and choose Edit ➤ Copy.

2. Select the calculator you need.

3. Choose Edit ➤ Paste. It is not necessary to clear the display first. The number will not appear on the display line until you enter an operator (+, –, *, and so forth.)

To Edit Your Entries

The tape display makes it possible to edit entries long after they have been made, even after they have scrolled off the screen.

1. Use the scroll bar to move to the entry that you want to change.

2. Double-click on that entry.

3. Enter the new number and click on the operator for the new number.

If the entry is in the Memo field, make sure the TXT function is toggled on. If the entry is on the active line, backspace to remove the number(s) or text.

To Open a Tape File

1. Select File ➤ Open Tape.

2. Type the filename in the File text box or use the drive, tree, and file lists to locate the file you want.

3. Select **OK** when finished.

To Print a Tape

1. If you want to print a different tape than the tape being displayed, follow the steps in *To Open a Tape File*.

2. Select File ➤ Print Tape.

To Save a Tape File

1. Select File ➤ Save Tape As.

2. Type the tape filename in the File text box.

3. Click on **OK** when finished.

To save changes to a tape file, choose File ➤ Save Tape.

DESKTOP EDITOR

The Desktop Editor is new to Version 2.0. In Version 1.0, the default editor is Windows Notepad. The Desktop Editor is a practical text editor with a variety of useful features.

STARTING DESKTOP EDITOR

To start Desktop Editor, choose one of the following options.

- Select Tools ➤ Desktop Editor.

- Select one or more files from a file pane and then select File ➤ Edit.

- Select File ➤ Run. Type in **DESKEDIT**. If you wish, you can specify the name of the file or files by typing in the filename with or without wildcards (* or ?). For example, to open all your Batch Builder batch files in separate windows, type in **DESKEDIT *.WBT** and press **Enter**.

OPENING, CLOSING, AND SAVING FILES

The Desktop Editor is a text editor with many specialized features for programmers. However, files can be opened and closed much as they are in a conventional word processor.

To Open a File

To open one or more files, choose from the following options.

- Select File ➤ Open. In the File Open dialog box, type in the name of the file you want to open, including the path. Or you may use the tree window to search for a particular file.

- Highlight a file in a file pane and click **Edit** on the button bar.

- Highlight one or more text files in a file pane and select File ➤ Edit.

- Pull down the File menu and select from the list of the four most recently opened files.

To Close a File

If the file has not been changed, you can close it by selecting File ➤ Close.

To Save a File

1. For a newly created file, select File ➤ Save As. The Save As dialog box will be opened and you can type in the file name as well as choose a different directory. To save changes to the existing file choose File ➤ Save.

2. Select **OK** to confirm your choice or **Cancel** to abandon the operation.

EDITING FILES

Once inside a file, Desktop Editor provides many options for manipulating text files.

To Copy Text to a File on Disk

1. Highlight the text you want to copy.

2. Select File ➤ Write Block.

3. In the Write Block dialog box, type in the name you want for the file or use the tree window to find a file you want to replace.

4. Click on **OK**.

To Copy Text from One Windows Document to Another

1. Highlight the text you want to copy.

2. Select Edit ➤ Copy.

3. Open the destination Windows document and position the cursor where you want the text to be placed.

4. Select Edit ➤ Paste from the menu of the document's application.

To Delete Text

Text can be deleted using one of the following options:

- Highlight the text you want to delete and press the **Del** key or select Edit ➤ Delete.

- Highlight the text you want to delete and select Edit ➤ Cut. With this choice, the text will be moved to the Clipboard.

- Press Alt-D to delete the current line.

- Press Ctrl-Del to delete the next word.

- Press Ctrl-Backspace to delete the previous word.

- Press Alt-K to delete all text from the cursor to the end of the current line.

To Cut and Paste Text

1. Highlight the text you want to move.

2. Select Edit ➤ Cut.

3. Move the cursor to the position where you want the text to appear, either in the same file or in another Windows document.

4. Select Edit ➤ Paste.

To Insert a File into the Current File

1. Position the cursor where you want to insert the file.

2. Select File ➤ Insert. The Insert File dialog box will open.

3. In the File text box, type in the name of the file you want to insert or use the tree and file panes to select a file.

4. Click on **OK** when you are finished.

To Record and Play a Macro

This macro facility is for simple sequences to be used during the current editing session. Only one macro can be stored at a time and it is lost when you leave the Desktop Editor. For permanent macros, see *Macro Builder*, below.

1. Select Edit ➤ Macro Builder.

2. Type in the keystrokes and perform the mouse movements that you want to record.

3. Select Edit ➤ Stop Recording Macro or press **F7**.

4. To play back the macro, select Edit ➤ Play Back Macro or press **F8**.

● **NOTE**   A macro built here is limited to a total of 256 keystrokes and menu selections and will not work inside dialog boxes.

To Reposition Text in Your Document

The following keystrokes can be used to move a line without moving the cursor:

Ctrl-T shifts the current line to the top of the window.

Ctrl-B moves the current line to the bottom of the window.

To Undo Changes

Changes can be reversed in two ways. To undo one change at a time, select Edit ➤ Undo. Each time you make this choice, the program will undo one editing change up to the number of levels specified under Editor Preferences (see *Configuring Desktop Editor*). You cannot undo operations any farther than the last save.

To undo all changes since the file was last saved, select File ➤ Revert.

● OPTIONS: EDIT MENU

Select All selects all text in the current file.

Time/Date inserts the current date and time at the cursor.

Word Wrap automatically moves the next word to the next line when you reach the right margin. This setting is for the current document only. To set it for all documents, see *Configuring Desktop Editor*.

Wrap Paragraph reformats the current paragraph after you have inserted or deleted text. Has no effect if Word Wrap is not toggled on.

COMPARING FILES

This function allows you to search for both similarities and differences in any two text files. If you are comparing files in document windows, the comparison will be made between the files as they are shown. The version on disk may be different if you have changed the files since you last saved.

To Compare Files

1. Select File ➤ Compare.
2. In the Compare dialog box, type in the names of the files to be compared or click on the prompt button to see the last ten files you've specified.

3. To compare the entire file, leave the Line setting at the default, Line 1. To start a comparison somewhere else in the file, enter a line number.

4. In the Display box, choose Horizontal to display one file above the other or Vertical for side-by-side display.

5. Click on **OK** to start.

The program will search to find differences. When a difference is found, the lines that do not match will be highlighted. A dialog box will open and you can choose to find the **Next Matching** lines or **Cancel**. If you select **Next Matching**, the next set of matching lines will be highlighted and you can then choose **Next Differences** or **Cancel**. The program will alternate finding matches and differences until the files are entirely scanned.

SEARCHING FILES

The Desktop Editor has very sophisticated search capabilities. You can look for a particular text string or you can locate expressions defined by a series of text wildcards.

To Search for a Text String

1. Select Search ➤ Find (or use the key combination Alt-S, F).

2. In the text box, enter the pattern you want to search for. Alternatively, click on the prompt button to see a list of recent choices.

3. Click on the **Next** button to start the search.

After the first occurrence of the pattern has been found, select Search ➤ Find Again or use the key combination Alt-S, A to find the next incidence. To search backward, click on the **Previous** button and then the **Next** button (Alt-S, A).

To Search for and Replace Text

1. Select Search ➤ Replace (Alt-S, R).

2. Enter the text you want to search for in the Search For text box.

3. In the Replace With text box, type in the new text. In both cases, you can click on the prompt button for a list of recent choices. If you clear the Confirm Changes check box, all changes will be made at once. With Confirm Changes checked, a dialog box will appear asking you to OK each change as it comes up.

4. Click on **OK** to start the search.

To Search Particular Files

1. Select Search ➤ Find Files Containing.

2. In the Pattern text box, type in the text you want to look for.

3. The directory to be searched will be shown in the Directory text field. To select another directory, click on the Directory button. In the Files text box, enter the name of the file you want to examine. Use wildcards or multiple file names separated by spaces. For example, key in ***.*** to search all the files in the directory, or ***.TXT *.DOC** to search files with the .TXT and .DOC extensions. Click on prompt buttons for lists of recent choices.

4. The List Found Files dialog box will open with the names of the files containing the search pattern. Double-click on a file name to open it. To return to the list, select Search ➤ List Found Files.

• SEARCH OPTIONS

Match Upper/Lower Case finds only exact matches to the cases specified in the text box.

Regular Expression allows you to use special codes, shown in Table IV.4, to customize your search.

Table IV.4: Regular Expressions

Character	Function
[chars]	Matches any of the characters between the brackets. [A–Z] matches any uppercase letter. [1–6] matches 1, 2, 3, 4, 5, or 6.
[~chars]	Matches any characters exept those that follow the tilde. [~0–9] matches any character that is not a number. [~] matches any character.
?	Matches any single character. ??? matches any three characters.
*	Matches zero or more of any character.
\	Next character is literal. \? searches for a question mark.
% or <	Matches the beginning of a line. <[A] matches any line that begins with the capital letter *A*.
$ or >	Matches the end of a line. [0–9]$ matches any line that ends with a number.
%$ or <>	Finds a blank line.
@	Matches zero or more occurences of the previous character
[A–Z][~]@	matches any word that starts with a capital letter.
\t	Finds a tab character.
\f	Finds a form feed.

● EXAMPLE

[0-9]??-[0-9]?-[0-9]??? finds any Social Security number.

PRINTING

Printing from the Desktop Editor employs features from Windows but also adds a few special formatting options.

To Print the Current File

Select File ➤ Print and the file will be automatically passed to the Windows Print Manager and printed from there.

To Select a Printer

If you have more than one printer, select File ➤ Printer Setup. The Printer Setup dialog box will open. You can select another printer or click on Setup to change the printer options.

To Set Up the Page Format

1. Select File ➤ Page Setup.

2. In the Page Setup dialog box, you can choose from the following options.

   Header: The default header is the full path and file name (*%f*) followed by the current date and time (*%d*). If you want a different line at the top of each page, type it in the Header text box. If you want no header, delete all characters in the Header box.

   Footer: The default footer is *Page* followed by the page number (*%p*). A different line of text can be typed into the Footer text box or you can remove all the characters from the text box to have no footer.

   Margins: Sets printed margins for your document. Units of measure are those set in the Windows Control Panel.

Font: Click on the Font button and select from the fonts
that appear in the Printer Font dialog box.

3.   Click on **OK** when finished.

CONFIGURING DESKTOP EDITOR

Configuration options can be set temporarily or permanently. Document Preferences are for the current document only, unless the Set
Default option is checked. Editor Preferences are permanent. Key Assignments can be either permanent or for the current session only.

To Set Document Preferences

Select Options ➤ Document Preferences. Set the options you want
and click on OK when finished.

● OPTIONS: DOCUMENT PREFERENCES

Tab Spacing specifies the number of characters you want between each tab stop.

Right Margin sets the right margin for word wrap.

Word Wrap turns on word wrap. If this box is clear, lines are
ended only when Enter is pressed.

Auto Indent causes the next line to start directly under the first
non-blank character on the previous line.

Expand Tabs With Spaces substitutes spaces for tab characters
in the saved document.

Save As Default Settings specifies that the settings you make
here are to be in effect for all future documents. If cleared, the
settings will be in effect for the current file only.

To Set Editor Preferences

Select Options ➤ Editor Preferences. Make your selections and click
on **OK** when you are finished.

• OPTIONS: EDITOR PREFERENCES

Font: By default the display is System Fixed Font. You can choose ANSI Fixed Font or OEM Fixed Font as well. The source of these fonts is found in the [boot] section of the SYSTEM.INI file.

Cursor: In this box you can choose how the cursor will appear on your screen. The cursor can be a block, underline, or vertical bar. Clear the Blinking check box if you want a steady cursor.

Autosave Every: You can set the program to automatically save your files after a set amount of time, after a set number of changes, or both. By default, the Autosave function is off. Enter the number of minutes between changes in the Autosave Every X minutes box. Enter the number of changes between saves in the Autosave Every X Changes box. To disable either or both functions, enter zeroes in the boxes.

Undo Levels: This setting determines how many levels of the Undo command can be performed. The default is 100. Lowering this number will decrease the amount of memory used by Desktop Editor.

Restore Session: Check this option to reopen the files that were open when you last exited Desktop Editor. This is useful if you edit the same files regularly.

Typing Replaces Selection: When you select text and start typing, the new characters replace the highlighted text. If you want the new characters to be inserted in front of the selected text, clear this check box.

Make Backup Files: By default, a backup file with the extension .BAK is made whenever you save a file. If you don't want automatic backup files, clear this check box.

File Locking: Check this box if you want your files to be inaccessible to other applications. To use this function, you must have the DOS program SHARE.EXE loaded before you start Windows.

Cut/Copy Current Line if No Text is Selected: If this box is checked, the current line will be selected when you use the Cut or Copy command. If you only want to Cut or Copy when text is selected, clear this box.

Remove Trailing Spaces: When this box is checked, the editor will discard any spaces or tabs at the end of a line.

To Set Key Assignments

Key Assignments lets you look up the currently assigned keystroke for an editor function as well as make your own assignments, save them for future use, and design custom keyboards.

1. Select Options ➤ Key Assignments.

2. Select the name of the function from the Function list. If the function already has a key assignment, it will appear in the Current Keys box.

3. Click on a key assignment in the Key list. If the keystroke already has a function assigned to it, it will appear in the Current Function box. Only the keystrokes on the list are acceptable.

4. Click on Assign ➤ OK to use this assignment for the current session only. Click on Assign ➤ Save ➤ OK to make the assignment permanent.

To remove an assignment, make the selections and click on Unassign ➤ OK (to remove the assignment for the current session only) or Unassign ➤ Save ➤ OK (to remove the assignment permanently).

To Use Menu Bar Accelerators

If you want to use the key combinations that are usually available on the menu bar, select Options ➤ Key Assignments and clear the Enable Menu Accelerators check box. The key combinations that are used to access the menus, such as Alt-F (File menu) can then be assigned to other functions. This will mean that you will need to use the mouse or the **Alt** key plus ← or → to access the menu bar.

To Create a Keyboard Configuration File

1. Make your choices in the Key Assignments dialog box.

2. Type in the name of the keyboard file using the .KEY extension in the Keyboard Configuration text box.

3. Click on Save ➤ OK.

To load a keyboard configuration file, open the Key Assignments dialog box. Type in the name of the file in the Keyboard Configuration text box and select Load.

DISK LABEL

Labeling a hard disk is a security measure designed to prevent accidental formatting. The format program in Norton Desktop for Windows and the regular DOS format will not format a labeled hard disk unless the label name is provided.

To Add or Change a Disk Label

1. Select Disk ➤ Label Disk.

2. In the dialog box, click on the prompt button to see a list of the drives on your system and their assigned labels, if any.

3. Select the drive and key in the label name in the New Label text box.

4. Select **OK** when you're finished.

To Delete a Disk Label

1. Select Disk ➤ Label Disk.

2. Click on the prompt button and select the drive.

3. Use the mouse to highlight the name in the New Label text box. Press **Delete**.

4. Select **OK** when you're finished.

DISKETTE FUNCTIONS

Norton Desktop for Windows allows you to format and copy diskettes in the Windows environment. All the new DOS 5.0 diskette functions are available here in a graphic, easy-to-use form.

To Format a Diskette

1. Select Disk ➤ Format Diskette.

2. Click on the prompt buttons at the side of the drop-down boxes to select one option from each of the following windows:

Diskette: Select the A drive or B drive.

Size: Select the size of the diskette being formatted.

Format Type: The *Safe* format uses its own formatting algorithm, which allows the recovery of data (using UnErase) in the event of accidental formatting. The *Quick* format is very fast because it rewrites the FAT table on the diskette; therefore it cannot be used on a previously unformatted diskette, though. A *Destructive* format is the same as a DOS format and erases the data completely and irrevocably.

3. Select any options that you want. Click on **OK** when you have made your choices. Select **OK** or **Cancel**.

● OPTIONS

Make Disk Bootable transfers DOS system files to the diskette so your computer can boot from them.

Save Unformat Information is available only when using the Quick format. Safe format does the save automatically and Destructive leaves nothing on the disk. Norton UnFormat can recover data from a diskette when unformat information has been saved.

Volume Label may be keyed in here, if desired.

To Copy a Diskette

1. Select Disk ➤ Copy Diskette.

2. Click on the prompt buttons to select the source and destination drives. Click on **OK**.

3. You will be prompted to insert the source diskette. Click **OK**.

4. You will then be prompted to insert the target diskette. If the target diskette is already formatted or contains files, a window opens with a warning message. Select **OK** if you want to go ahead. Select **Swap Disks** if you want to change the target diskette or **Cancel** to abandon the operation.

5. When you are finished copying, you will be asked if you want to make another copy of the source diskette. Select **Yes** if you do or **No** if you want to exit.

● **NOTE**   A diskette can be copied to a diskette of identical configuration only. If you attempt to copy a diskette of one capacity to a diskette of a different capacity, you will get an error message. You can, however, do a file copy by opening the drive window for the source diskette, highlighting all the files, and dragging the file icon to the target diskette's drive icon.

ICON EDITOR

The Icon Editor is a complete icon management tool. It lets you work with individual icon files, icons inside executable files, and libraries of icons. With the Icon Editor, you can do following:

• Create or change existing individual icons

• Create, change, or replace program icons

• Create, delete, or change individual icons in icon libraries

• Create or change entire icon libraries

ABOUT ICONS

Both Windows and Norton Desktop for Windows use icons to visually identify programs. Icons can be stored as individual .ICO files, within the application program's file itself, or in icon libraries. By default, Norton Desktop for Windows uses icon libraries with the .NIL extension. The Icon Editor lets you edit and work with icons in all three places.

Icons can be associated with an application program or with any object in the desktop.

THE ICON EDITOR

To start the Icon Editor, select Tools ➤ Icon Editor or double-click on its icon in the Norton Desktop for Windows group. You'll see a window like the one shown in Figure IV.5.

Parts of the Icon Editor

The parts of the Icon Editor are as follows:

Workspace	The workspace is the main area of the Icon Editor. It consists of a 32× 32 grid, each square of which represents a pixel in the icon.
Icon display	The Icon display shows the current icon in the Workspace, including all edits.
Tools palette	The Tools palette contains eight tool buttons with the drawing tools that are used to edit the icon in the Workspace. Click on one of the tool buttons to select its tool.
Brush Size palette	The Brush Size palette has four buttons for selecting different brush sizes. The four available sizes are these: 1×1 pixel, 2×2 pixels, 3×3 pixels, and 4×4 pixels.

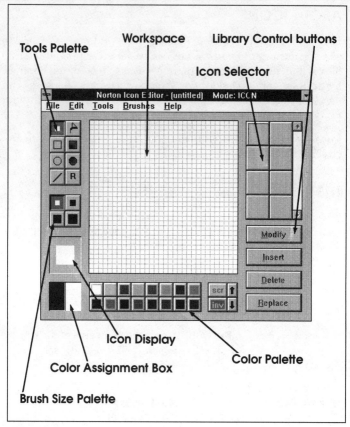

Figure IV.5: The Icon Editor

Color Assignment box	The current color assignments for the right and left mouse buttons are shown in the Color Assignment box. An *s* or an *i* in the box indicates that it is a screen color or its inverse. If neither an *s* nor an *i* appears, that indicates that it is a "fast" color. (See *How To Select Colors* later in this entry.)

Color palette   The Color palette shows the available colors. At the right of the palette there are the Screen Color box, the Inverse Color box, and two Spin buttons, which cycle through the colors. The Screen Color box shows the current screen color while the Inverse Color box shows a pre-assigned contrasting color.

Library
Control
buttons   The four Library Control buttons are Modify, Insert, Delete, and Replace. They are used to move icons to and from the workspace and to insert or delete icons from a library. When editing individual icons or executable files, only the Modify and Replace buttons are available.

Icon Selector   The Icon Selector is a scrollable box with eight buttons displaying the icons in the library or executable file.

THE DRAWING TOOLS

The drawing tools are used to edit the icon in the workspace. The eight tools are shown in Figure IV.6. They function as follows:

Brush   The Brush tool allows you to change the color of the pixels in the workspace either by clicking on the pixel or by dragging the pointer over an area. The size of the brush is controlled by the Brush palette, and the color of the brush is controlled by the Color palette.

Filler   The Filler tool fills a region with the color assigned to the left or right mouse button. It will fill a contiguous area, including the pixel on which you click.

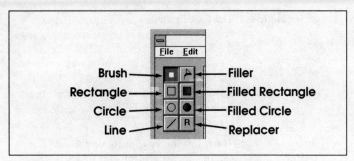

Figure IV.6: The Tool palette has eight drawing tools.

Rectangle	The Rectangle tool draws an outline of a rectangle in the workspace. Click on one corner of the rectangle and drag the pointer to the opposite corner.
Filled Rectangle	The Filled Rectangle tool works the same as the Rectangle tool, except that the inside region of the rectangle is filled with the assigned mouse button color.
Circle	The Circle tool draws an approximation of an ellipse inside an imaginary rectangle. Click on one corner of the imaginary rectangle and then drag the pointer to the opposite corner.
Filled Circle	The Filled Circle tool works the same as the Circle tool, except that the inside region of the ellipse is filled with the assigned mouse button color.
Line	The Line tool draws a line in the workspace. Click on one end of the line and then drag the pointer to the end of the line.

Replacer   The Replacer tool works like the Brush
                        tool, except that it replaces all the pixels of
                        one color with another color.
                        The replacement color is the color assigned
                        to the button used, and the color replaced
                        is the color assigned to the other button.
                        This tool is very handy for changing the
                        color of one pixel without affecting any of
                        the pixels around it.

HOW TO SELECT COLORS

There are two kinds of colors in the Icon Editor. Screen and Inverse
colors and Fast colors. Screen and Inverse colors can be changed by
using the two Spin buttons to cycle through the palette. Fast colors
do not change once they have been painted.

- To set the left mouse button to a Fast color, move the
  cursor to the color on the Color palette and click on the
  left mouse button.

- To set the right mouse button, repeat the procedure, but
  use the right mouse button.

- To set a mouse button to a Screen color, move the cursor to
  the **scr** button and click the mouse button.

- To set a mouse button to the Inverse color, position the cursor on the **inv** button and click on the mouse button.

- To change the Screen and Inverse colors, click the left
  mouse button on one of the spin buttons to the right of
  the **scr** and **inv** buttons. These cycle through the color
  pairs in opposite directions.

WORKING WITH INDIVIDUAL ICONS

Icon Editor allows you to change icons. You can create new icons
either by modifying existing ones or by creating them from scratch.
New icons can then be saved as individual icons, or as part of a
library of icons.

To Create an Icon

1. Start Icon Editor by double-clicking on its icon or by selecting Tools ➤ Icon Editor. If you are already in the Editor, select File ➤ New.

2. If you select File ➤ New, a dialog box will open. Select **Icon** to work on an individual icon.

3. The workspace will clear and the Brush tool will be selected.

4. Draw the icon.

5. Click on the **Replace** button to move the icon in the workspace to the Icon Selector.

6. Select File ➤ Save or File ➤ Save As to save the icon in an .ICO file or an .NIL file if you are creating a new library (and if you chose Icon Library in step 2 above.).

● **NOTE**   To undo any changes made to the icon in the workspace since the last time you changed tools, select Edit ➤ Undo.

To Edit an Existing Icon

1. Start Icon Editor by selecting Tools ➤ Icon Editor or by clicking on its icon. Select File ➤ Open.

2. Select the icon to be edited.

3. Click on the **Modify** button to move the icon into the workspace and then select the drawing tools and colors desired.

4. When you have finished editing the icon, click on the **Replace** button to overwrite the original.

5. To save the modified icon in an individual .ICO file, select Export Icon, Save, or Save As from the File menu. Selecting Export Icon or Save will bring up a dialog box. Key in the *filename* for the modified icon and then select **OK**. **Warning:** Selecting Save will result in overwriting the original icon with the one now in the workspace.

WORKING WITH ICON LIBRARIES

Norton Desktop for Windows allows you to create and work with libraries of icons. A library of icons is a file that contains one or more icons. With Norton Desktop, these files have the extension .NIL. Working with icons in these libraries is similar to working with individual icons, except that you can add or delete icons from the libraries, and import or export icons to individual .ICO files.

To Import an Icon

1. Open the library that you want to modify by selecting File ➤ Open. The Open dialog box will be displayed.

2. Specify in the File Type box whether to import an icon from an existing library file, an executable file, or an individual icon file.

3. Select the file from which to import.

4. Select the icon to import from the Icon Selector button bar near the bottom of the dialog box.

5. Select **OK** to import the icon to the workspace or **Cancel** to abort the operation.

To Export an Icon

1. Move the icon to be exported to the workspace.

2. Select File ➤ Export Icon.

3. The Export Icon dialog box will open. Key in the file name for the icon.

4. Select **OK** to save the icon to an .ICO file or **Cancel** to cancel the operation.

To Delete an Icon from an Icon Library

1. Click on the icon to be deleted in the Icon Selector.

2. Click on the **Delete** button. The icon will be deleted immediately from the Icon Selector.

3. Select File ➤ Save to make the change permanent.

To Insert an Icon in an Icon Library

1. Open the desired Icon Library or select File ➤ New to start a new library.

2. Draw the icon in the workspace or import it from another file using File ➤ Import Icon.

3. Click on the **Insert** button. The icon in the workspace will be inserted into the library in front of the current icon.

4. Select File ➤ Save to make the change permanent.

WORKING WITH ICONS IN EXECUTABLE FILES

Icons can be embedded in executable files. The Icon Editor allows you to change these icons or to replace them with icons of your own. You cannot, however, change the number of icons in the executable file.

To Edit an Icon in an Executable File

1. Select File ➤ Open.

2. Select the Executable radio button.

3. Select the file to edit.

4. Select **OK** to bring the file into the Icon Editor or **Cancel** to cancel the operation.

5. Select the icon to change in the Icon Selector.

6. Click on the **Modify** button to move the icon to the workspace.

7. Edit the icon.

8. Click on the **Replace** button to replace the icon with the edited icon in the workspace.

9. Select File ➤ Save to make the changes permanent.

To Replace an Icon in an Executable File

To replace an icon in an executable file with one from another source, such as an icon library, follow the first five steps in *To Edit an Icon in an Executable File,* above. Then follow these steps:

1. Select File ➤ **Import**.

2. Select the file and icon to import to the workspace. (See *To Import an Icon,* above).

3. Click on the **Replace** button to replace the icon with the icon you imported to the workspace.

4. Select File ➤ Save to make the changes permanent.

KEYFINDER

The KeyFinder is a handy utility that helps you to determine keystrokes to insert special characters into your current Windows application quickly and easily. You can use either the keyboard or a mouse. To start KeyFinder, either select Tools ➤ Keyfinder or double-click on its icon in the Norton Desktop for Windows group window. You will see the default KeyFinder window, as shown in Figure IV.7.

The KeyFinder window is composed of the Character Table, arranged in either rows or columns, the Keystroke Information box, the Sample Text box, the Available Fonts box, and the Font Size box.

To Find a Character Code

1. Choose the font. (See *To Change Font,* below.)

2. Click on the character or symbol desired.

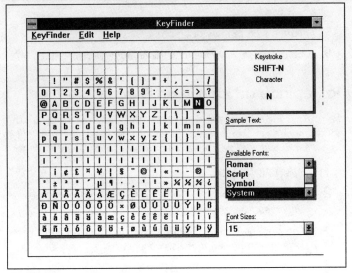

Figure IV.7: The KeyFinder window

3. The character will be displayed in the Keystroke Information box, along with the keystroke(s) used to create it.

● EXAMPLE

To find the keystrokes for the copyright symbol, in the System font, select System in the Available Fonts box, then click on the © symbol. The copyright symbol is displayed in the Keystroke Information box, along with the keystrokes to create it in the System font: Alt 169.

● **NOTE** To key extended ASCII characters (those greater than ASCII code 127) in most Windows applications, first make sure that NumLock is on. Then hold down the **Alt** key while entering the number shown in the Keystroke Information box. When you release the **Alt** key, the symbol will appear.

To Insert Multiple Characters into the Current Windows Application

1. Select the font being used by the application in the Available Fonts box. (See *To Change Font*, below.)

2. Select the characters to insert into the application by double-clicking on them. They will appear in the Sample Text box.

3. Highlight the characters in the Sample Text box by dragging across them with the mouse.

4. Copy the characters to the clipboard. Select Edit ➤ Copy or Edit ➤ Cut. Alternately, press **Ctrl-Insert** to copy the characters or **Shift-Delete** to cut them to the clipboard.

5. Change to the application.

6. Paste the characters into the application. This is usually Edit ➤ Paste or **Shift-Insert**.

● **NOTE**   The actual keystrokes are pasted into the application, not the formatted characters. Make sure to select the font and size being used before performing the paste operation.

● **OPTIONS: EDIT MENU**

Lower Case changes all the characters in the Sample Text box to lowercase.

Upper Case changes all the characters in the Sample Text box to uppercase.

Copy Cell copies the current cell in the Character Table into the Sample Text box. This has the same effect as double-clicking on the cell.

To Change Font

1. Click on the scroll bar arrows in the Available Fonts box until the desired font becomes visible.

2. Click on the font name. The Character Table will change to show the new font.

To Change Font Size

1.   Select the font in the Available Fonts box.

2.   Click on the prompt button of the Font Sizes box to show the available font sizes.

3.   Scroll through the font sizes and select the one desired. This will be the size shown in the Keystroke Information box, if Real Font Size is toggled on.

● OPTIONS: KEYFINDER MENU

Swap Orientation changes the Character Table from row orientation to column orientation.

Real Font Size shows the actual size of characters in the Keystroke Information box.

Show ASCII shows ASCII code for nonprinting characters.

Sample Text toggles the Sample Text box display.

Programmer Mode changes the Keystroke Information box to show additional information about the character selected, including the following details:

• Keystroke

• Character

• Decimal equivalent for the character

• Hex equivalent for the character

• Octal equivalent for the character

• Type of font selected

• Font style selected

Programmer Mode also changes the Character Table to show a hex number grid on the outside and eliminates the Font Size box. See Figure IV.8.

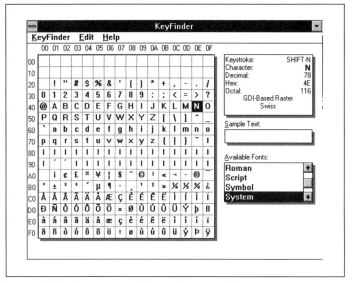

Figure IV.8: Programmer Mode shows additional useful information for programmers.

THE MACRO BUILDER

Version 2.0 of Norton Desktop for Windows has added an important new tool for those who want to automate and customize repetitive tasks in Windows. The Macro Builder lets you record the keystrokes required to perform a task and recall them with only a few keystrokes. The macro is recorded as Norton Windows Batch Language *SendKey* statements (See *Part Five: The Norton Windows Batch Language*), which can then be edited and combined with other batch language commands to make useful and powerful batch files, automating even complicated tasks.

It is important to keep in mind the limitations of the Macro Builder. With one exception, it can record only keystrokes. Mouse movements and actions are ignored, except you can use the mouse to activate a window on your desktop by clicking on it. This is recorded as a WinActivate command. Also, unlike Batch Builder's .WBT files, which are full programs, the Macro Builder's .WBM files are program fragments that are dependent on the context of the desktop at the time they are recorded. If the desktop changes, the keystrokes may end up being passed to a completely different application when you run the macro. However, since you can easily combine Macro Builder with Batch Builder files, the combination provides a powerful and flexible utility.

To Record a Macro

1. Open the Macro Builder by choosing Tools ➤ Macro Builder or double-clicking its icon if you have placed it on the desktop.

2. Click on **Record** to begin recording keystrokes. (Note: You can bypass this step by checking the disable box or by editing your NDW.INI file in the Windows subdirectory to add the following line to the [Defaults] section:

   MacroBuilderPrompt=0

3. If the Macro Builder is already open and running, **Ctrl Shift-Home** will start a recording.

4. Perform the keystrokes you want to record.

5. To stop recording, press **Ctrl-Shift-End**.

6. The Save Macro Builder As dialog box will open. Key in a file name for your macro. (The default extension is .WBM.)

7. A dialog box will open asking if you want to add the macro you just saved to the Launch List. Select **Yes** if you want to make this macro available from any window, even if zoomed.

• EXAMPLE

Here is a Macro Builder macro that will change your wallpaper to the next wallpaper available (alphabetically). Add it to your Launch List, and it will be there whenever you get tired of your current wallpaper. You can even assign it to a single keystroke combination for instant access.

```
; Recorded Macro
WinActivate("Quick Access")
SendKey('!frcontrol.exe{ENTER}d{ENTER}!f{DOWN}{ENTER}! c')
; End Recorded Macro
```

To Play Back a Macro

You can play back a macro using any of the methods for launching a file. If you have added it to your launch list, you can launch it from there, drag the file onto the desktop, add it to a group window, launch it from a drive window, or add it to a custom menu. For more information, see *Part Two: Configuring the Desktop*.

To Edit a Macro

When you create a macro, it frequently needs a little cleaning up. To edit a macro you have just recorded, click once on the Macro Builder icon to activate its control menu, and select **Edit Macro Builder File**. This will open the Batch Builder with the most recent macro file ready for editing. If you find that an older macro needs modification, choose Tools ➤ Batch Builder to open the Batch Builder and open the file you want to edit. You can also use any ASCII text editor to edit these files.

To Combine Macros with the Batch Language

Perhaps the most powerful and useful way to use the Macro Builder is to record a series of keystrokes that you will then combine with Norton Windows Batch Language commands to make an intelligent batch file. Here, the goal is to use the Macro Builder to capture the keystrokes being passed to the application. This takes a bit of practice and editing to get right, but with experience you can develop sophisticated programs to handle even the most complex tasks.

• EXAMPLE

While not by any means as sophisticated as other possible examples, here is a batch file that will prompt the user for a file name, open WordPerfect for Windows with that file, and switch the screen to draft mode, my preferred editing screen. If WordPerfect is already open, it will activate it and open the file.

```
; This macro first prompts the user for a file name
; then loads WordPerfect for Windows if it isn't
; already loaded, and opens up a file. In this case,
; defaults to MACROED.CH4, but could be anything.
filevar = AskLine("WordPerfect FileName", "What File
Would You Like to Edit", "macroed.ch4")
filevar = StrCat("d:\wp51\ndw\", filevar)
IF WinExist("WordPerfect")==@FALSE THEN goto OPENWP
WinActivate("WordPerfect")
SendKey('!fo%filevar%')
SendKey('{ENTER}')
; If file is already open, next line is necessary
SendKey('{ESCAPE}{ESCAPE}')
goto DRAFT
:OPENWP
RunZoom("d:\wpw\wpwin.exe", filevar)
:DRAFT
SendKey('!vd')
```

NETWORK CONNECTIONS

If you are already signed onto a network, you can disconnect and reconnect individual network drives.

To Connect a Network Drive

1. Select Disk ➤ Connect Net Drive.

2. A Network Connections or Connect Network Drive dialog box will open depending on your network.

3. Select the name of the server and network path (you may have to type in this information) and enter your password.

4. If your network supports a browse feature, the **Browse** button will be activated and you can search for the network drive you want.

5. When you are finished, click on **OK** (or a similar button, such as **Connect**).

To Disconnect a Network Drive

1. Select Disk ➤ Disconnect Net Drive.

2. In the dialog box, select the network drive you wish to disconnect.

3. Click on **OK** (or similar button, such as **Disconnect**, depending on your network).

NORTON ANTIVIRUS

In Version 2.0 of Norton Desktop for Windows, Symantec has added the full version of the Norton AntiVirus (NAV) program. NAV is simple and easy to use, providing excellent protection against all known viruses, as well as against those not yet discovered. Regular, free updates to the virus definitions are available from the Symantec BBS or in the Norton Utilities area of CompuServe (see *To Update Virus Definitions*, below). NAV also has an intercept mode, which allows new viruses to be detected, even if they are not yet part of virus definitions in the main program, the Anti-Virus Clinic.

NORTON ANTIVIRUS CLINIC

The Norton AntiVirus Clinic provides the primary interface for the user to check files, directories, and disks for viral infections, as well as to repair any damage.

To Scan a Drive or Drives

Norton AntiVirus will scan one or more drives, including net-worked drives, to search for the "signature" of any of the viruses it knows. If you have enabled the option to check for unknown viruses, it will also check to see if any executable files have been modified since the last time you inoculated the drive.

1. Choose Scan ➤ Drive.

2. The Scan Drives dialog box will open.

3. Choose the drive or drives to scan for infections. Either choose individual drives using the Drives list box or click on the check boxes to select multiple drives. Here are your options:

   - **All Floppy Drives** selects all floppy drives installed on this computer.

   - **All Local Drives** selects all local drives, except for floppy drives.

   - **All Network Drives** selects all network drives that are connected. (Access to this option may be turned off using Options ➤ Clinic).

4. If this is the first scan of the current session, NAV will first scan the computer's memory for any resident viruses.

5. Once NAV has scanned all of the drives you have selected, it will open the Scan Results dialog box and report the number of files scanned, and the number of viruses found. If viruses were found, the option buttons for **Repair**, **Delete**, and **Reinoculate** will now be available.

To Scan a Subdirectory or File

Norton AntiVirus will scan a file or directory to search for the "signature" of any viruses it knows. If you have enabled the option to check for unknown viruses, it will also check to see if any executable files have been modified since the last time you inoculated them.

1. Choose Scan ➤ File or Scan ➤ Directory to scan a file or a directory.

2. Select the file or directory to scan. Click **OK** to scan the file or directory.

3. If this is the first scan of the current session, NAV will first scan the computer's memory for any resident viruses.

4. Once NAV has scanned the file or directory you selected, it will open the Scan Results dialog box and report the number of files scanned and the number of viruses found. If viruses were found, the option buttons for **Repair**, **Delete**, and **Reinoculate** will now be available.

When a Virus Is Found

Norton AntiVirus will repair most infected files it finds, as well as repairing the boot sector and partition table when they are infected. If NAV finds an infected file (or files) while scanning for a virus in the boot sector or partition table of the disk being scanned, it will report the files or areas infected. At this point, you can choose to repair the file or area, delete the file, or reinoculate it if NAV has reported a possible unknown virus. If the file is no longer required, click on the **Delete** button. NAV will ask you to confirm the deletion. Click **Delete** to delete just this file or **Delete All** to delete all similarly infected files. A final warning box will give you one last chance to cancel without deleting the file. Click **Delete** again to complete the deletion.

• **WARNING** Files deleted by Norton AntiVirus are completely and irrevocably deleted. They can not be recovered by the undelete or unerase utilities.

If NAV has reported a virus in the boot sector of a floppy, in the partition table of a hard disk, or in a file that you still need and cannot easily replace, click **Repair**. NAV will open the Repair Files dialog box. Choose **Repair** to repair just the one file or **Repair All** to repair all infected files.

Finally, if the option is turned on to detect unknown viruses, NAV might report that a file may contain an unknown virus. If the file has been updated or otherwise changed since last inoculated, this will most likely be a false report; but if not, NAV may have just saved you from a disaster with a new virus strain. If you are absolutely certain that the file is safe and that it has been changed since the disk was last inoculated, click **Reinoc** to reinoculate the file. The Reinoculate Files dialog box will open. Click **Reinoc** to reinoculate only the single file or click **Reinoc All** to reinoculate all files reported as possibly being infected with an unknown virus. If you have any doubts about the file or have reason to suspect the file is infected, click **Delete** to delete the file. Unfortunately, Norton AntiVirus cannot repair a file infected with a virus it does not have in its definition list.

To Update Virus Definitions

Norton AntiVirus can only provide complete protection and repair capabilities against viruses for which it has definitions. Since new viruses are continually being introduced, it is important to keep Norton AntiVirus current. Symantec provides several methods for obtaining current definitions to update NAV. The choices are:

- The Symantec BBS, which provides current complete and update definition files. This can be accessed at 2400 baud or 9600 baud depending on your modem and communications software. The number for 2400 baud is **(408) 973-9598** and for 9600 baud **(408) 973-9834**.

- CompuServe. The NAV-IBM Library section of the Norton Utilities Forum also provides current complete and update definition files. Log onto CompuServe using your normal procedures and at any ! prompt type **GO NORUTIL** to reach the Norton Utilities Forum.

- Faxline. You can get a fax of the new virus definitions by calling **(310) 575-5018** from a touch-tone phone. Instructions and assistance for the Faxline are available by calling **(310) 477-2707**.

- Virus Definition Update Disk Service, which provides updated definitions for a nominal fee. (Currently $12.00 plus shipping, handling, and taxes.) You can order disks by calling **(800) 343-4714 ext. 756**.

Once you have the new definition file, you can update your copy of Norton AntiVirus.

1. Open the Norton AntiVirus Clinic by choosing Tools ➤ Norton AntiVirus from the Desktop menu or by double-clicking the Norton AntiVirus tool icon.

2. Choose Definitions ➤ Modify List or Definitions ➤ Load from File, depending on whether you have a hard copy of the new definitions or a .DEF file.

3. If you are modifying the list based on hard copy of the new definitions, the Modify List dialog box will open. Select **Add** to open the Add Virus Definition dialog box and type in the new definition. Click **OK** when you have finished entering the definition, and then click **OK** to accept the changes. Depending on which version of the AntiVirus Intercept you are using, the new definitions may not take effect until you reboot.

4. If you are updating Norton AntiVirus by loading the definitions from a file, the Load from File dialog box will open. Use the browse boxes to locate and select the new definition file and then click **OK** to load the new definitions into Norton AntiVirus. Depending on the version of the AntiVirus Intercept you are using, the new definitions may not take effect until you reboot.

To Inoculate against Unknown Viruses

Norton AntiVirus can detect changes in an executable file, which may indicate that they have become infected by a virus. This is even true for viruses it doesn't have definitions for. In order to check for unknown viruses, however, you must inoculate the disk so that NAV can detect the change.

1. Choose Options ➤ Global and check the Detect Unknown Viruses and Auto Inoculate boxes.

2. Scan the drive you want to inoculate, and Norton will automatically inoculate the files on that drive while it is scanning them for currently defined viruses.

To Uninoculate a Drive

If you update the programs on a drive, the inoculation data for that drive becomes outdated and will give false reports of possible virus infection. To correct this, you need to uninoculate the drive and then reinoculate it. It is best to do this when you have recently updated your virus definitions so that you are unlikely to accidentally inoculate a new virus against being infected by another new virus.

1. Choose Tools ➤ Uninoculate.

2. Select the drive(s) to uninoculate.

3. Click **OK** to begin the uninoculation.

4. If NAV was successful in uninoculating the drive(s), the Uninoculate Results information box will open. If it was unable to uninoculate the drive, usually because the drive was not inoculated, a warning box will inform you of the failure.

● OPTIONS: CLINIC

Allow Repair permits the user to select repair of infected files when Scan detects a virus.

Allow Delete permits the user to select deletion of infected files when Scan detects a virus.

Allow Reinoc permits the user to select reinoculation of files that have been reported as having a possible unknown virus. *Use this option with caution!*

Allow Cancel permits the user to cancel out of the Scan Results dialog box, even if a virus has been detected.

Allow Repair All permits the user to select a wholesale repair of multiple infected files.

Allow Delete All permits the user to delete all infected files when multiple files are affected.

Allow Reinoc All permits the user to simultaneously reinoculate all files that have been reported as having a possible unknown virus. *Use this option with extreme caution!*

Allow Scanning of Network Drives permits the user to scan all drives on a network, not just local ones.

● OPTIONS: INTERCEPT

Enable Beep Alert sounds a distinctive beep when a virus is encountered.

Enable Popup Alert displays an information box that describes the virus detected and optionally permits the user to use the file. The length of time this popup box stays on screen can be entered in the Seconds to Display Alert Box text box. An entry of 0 seconds will leave the box displayed until it is acknowledged.

Enable Log to File logs all virus reports to a file. Enter the file name for this log in the text box.

Allow Proceed allows the user to load an infected program after acknowledging the popup box.

Allow Reinoculate allows the user to reinoculate a file that is reported to have an unknown virus. *Use this option with caution!*

● OPTIONS: GLOBAL

Detect Unknown Viruses uses inoculation data to determine if an executable file has changed.

Auto Inoculate automatically stores inoculation data for each file the first time it is accessed. Scanning a file will cause it to be inoculated.

Scan Executables Only scans executable files only. Data files are ignored.

Network Inoculation Directory tells Norton AntiVirus where on the local drives to store the inoculation data for networked drives.

Virus Alert Custom Message allows you to have your own message in the popup box when Norton AntiVirus detects a virus.

• OPTIONS: PASSWORD

This allows you to set a password on all the other options to prevent unauthorized users from modifying the program options.

NORTON VIRUS INTERCEPTS

Norton AntiVirus comes with three memory-resident antivirus programs, which enable it to detect a virus before it infects other files. The programs are NAV_.SYS, NAV&.SYS /B, and NAV&.SYS. In order to provide protection against an infection spreading from its source, one of these should be loaded as a device driver in your CONFIG.SYS file.

```
DEVICE=C:\NDW\NAV_.SYS
DEVICE=C:\NDW\NAV&.SYS /B
DEVICE=C:\NDW\NAV&.SYS
```

Whichever of these device drivers you choose, it should be loaded as early in your CONFIG.SYS file as possible to provide maximum protection. If you use QEMM or another memory manager that permits programs to be loaded into high memory, however, the device driver line must come *after* the line that loads the memory manager.

The first option, NAV_.SYS, uses approximately 38K of memory, but provides the most comprehensive protection. Each application is scanned when it is launched, and files are scanned when they are copied. It also provides protection against boot sector and partition-table viruses.

The second option, NAV&.SYS /B, uses approximately 4K of memory and provides the best compromise between protection and size. It scans applications when they are launched and can detect boot-sector viruses on floppy drives.

The third option, NAV&.SYS, uses only 1K of memory, but will scan only when an application is launched. It will not detect boot-sector viruses on infected floppies.

NORTON BACKUP

Norton Desktop for Windows includes Norton Backup for Windows, a full-featured, flexible backup program that can be configured easily for novice or advanced users alike. Unlike many backup programs, Norton Backup for Windows operates in the Windows environment and can run in the background while you continue working on other tasks in the foreground. In Version 2.0, it supports several commonly used tape drives, including QIC-40 and QIC-80 types.

● **WARNING!** *Do not attempt to run any other program that uses the floppy-disk controller while using Backup. Data loss or a system crash are very likely if another program tries to use one of the floppy-disk drives while Backup is running.*

USING NORTON BACKUP THE FIRST TIME

Before Backup can run on your computer, it needs to know what kind of floppy and tape drives you have, and how your computer responds to certain commands. To get this information, the first time you start Backup it will automatically run a series of tests to determine how your hardware operates and it will check to make sure that its options are correctly set to ensure reliable backups. It is strongly recommended that you complete all of these tests before attempting to make backups.

To Backup the First Time

1. Click on the **Backup** icon or select Tools ➤ Backup.

2.   An information box will pop up, advising you that the compatibility tests have not been run yet. Select **OK** to proceed.

3.   Another information box will open telling you that your system is not yet configured. It will ask you if you want to configure automatically. Select **Yes** to proceed.

4.   Backup will next try to determine what kind of floppy-disk drives you have on your computer. First it will pop up an information box telling you to remove any floppy-disks from their drives. Do so and select **OK** in this box. A message box will open showing the configuration Backup has found. Select **OK** to proceed.

5.   If you have a tape drive and there is a tape in it, an information box opens asking you to remove the tape so the driver can be configured. Remove the tape and select **OK**. Another information box opens displaying the tape-drive type found. Select **OK** to proceed.

6.   Next, Backup will run a small compatibility test of your floppy-disk drives. This test does a two-disk backup of files and then compares the backed-up files against the originals. Select which drive to back up and then select **Start** to begin. A message box will pop up advising you not to allow any other programs to use the floppy-disk drives during this test. Click **OK** to proceed.

7.   Follow the prompts to run the backup and compare. Note that if you change disks within 15 seconds of the initial prompt, Backup will detect the change automatically.

8.   If you have a tape drive, Backup will next perform a similar small backup and compare to the tape drive. Again, select **Start** to begin, and then acknowledge the warning about simultaneous floppy-disk drive use.

9.   Finally, when the tests have concluded successfully, you can adjust any of the configuration options listed below.

• **NOTE** In Version 1.0, the sequence of steps is slightly different, and you will not be offered tape as an option, but the general intent is the same—to automatically configure Backup for your computer and to insure that backups can be reliably performed and restored. Just follow the prompts to complete the configuration and compatibility tests.

CONFIGURATION

To open the Configure window, click on the **Configure** button on the button bar (under the menu bar). This will allow you to make changes to the program level, floppy- and tape-drive type, disk-logging method, catalog-file path, and DMA speed. Any changes made here will apply to all operations in Backup.

Also, if you change any of your hardware after the initial installation and running of Backup, you should rerun the following configuration tests by clicking on the appropriate buttons.

• **OPTIONS: CONFIDENCE TESTS**

> **Floppy Configuration** allows you to reconfigure your floppy-disk drives, either manually or automatically. Options for each floppy-disk drive are:
>
> **Not Installed**
> **360 Kb 5¼**
> **720 Kb 5¼**
> **720 Kb 3½**
> **1.2 Mb 5¼**
> **1.44 Mb 3½**
>
> **Auto Tape Configure** automatically detects the presence and type of tape drive.
>
> **Compatibility Test** runs a backup and compare test to ensure dependable backups to the tape or floppy-disk drive of your choice.
>
> **Configuration Tests** (*Version 1.0*) tests the Fast DMA option and Disk Change detection.

• OPTIONS: PROGRAM LEVEL

Preset governs all options within the Backup, Compare, and Restore windows, except the drive to back up to or to restore/compare from.

Basic allows limited access to changing options within the Backup, Compare, and Restore windows.

Advanced allows full access to all options within the Backup, Compare, and Restore windows.

• OPTIONS: DISK LOG STRATEGY

Fastest works with most disk drives, but may not work with networked or substituted drives.

Most compatible works with all DOS devices and requires less memory than Fastest option.

• OPTIONS: DMA OPERATIONS

Fastest works with most disk drives but may not work with networked or substituted drives.

Most compatible works with all DOS devices and requires less memory than the Fastest option.

• OPTIONS: CATALOG FILE PATH

Key in the path to the location where you want Backup to store its catalog files. By default, these are in the same directory as Norton Desktop for Windows. They are also stored on the last disk in each set.

Version 1.0: Some of these options are in slightly different places and there are no tape drive options, but they all function in the same manner and have the same meaning as in Version 2.0.

THE BACKUP WINDOW

Norton Backup allows you a wide range of ways to handle backups. You can preconfigure your backups and run them automatically by adding parameters to the command line; then place the icon on your desktop to invoke backup manually at the end of the day or have Scheduler automatically run your backups for you.

You can create a variety of predefined setup files that back up different groups of files or you can interactively select the files to back up and then store them in a new setup file if you wish.

In addition, you can control the number and type of possible options for each backup, from virtually none (except for choosing a predefined set of files) with the program level set to Preset, to a full range of options for compression technique, format type, and so forth with the program level set to Advanced. Finally, you can back up files by highlighting them in a Drive Window and dragging them to the Backup icon on the desktop.

Types of Backups

There are three basic types of backups. They are:

- Full
- Incremental
- Differential

In addition, there are copy versions of the Full and Incremental backup types that do not change the archive bit of the files that are backed up, nor do they affect the backup cycle settings. These two options are useful primarily as means of transferring files between computers and will not be discussed again.

A Full backup is one made of all the files that you select. This can be all the files on the hard disk (a total backup), all the files in a particular drive or directory, or some other reasonable subset of the files on your hard disk. A Full backup turns off the archive bit on the backed-up files and begins a backup cycle. You can save the set of files selected for backup and re-use them later as a backup set.

An Incremental backup includes all the files in the set of files that have changed since your last Full or Incremental backup. An Incremental backup turns off the archive bit of each file that has been backed up. In the event of disaster to your hard disk, you must restore the Full backup set and *all* Incremental backup sets. Do not re-use incremental diskettes between Full backups, because a complete restore requires the full set plus *all* the incrementals.

A Differential backup includes all the files in a set of files that have changed since the last Full backup. A Differential backup does not turn off the archive bit. In order to restore files to your hard disk, you need restore only the last Full backup plus the most recent Differential backup. You can re-use all differential backup diskettes except the most recent, unless you want to maintain multiple versions of the changed files.

Program Level

There are three program levels for Backup: Preset, Basic, and Advanced. In the Backup window, these control the number and type of options that are available to the user. The program level is set in the Configure window.

● OPTIONS: PRESET

The only options available in the Backup window at the Preset level are the setup file to use, which is selected using the Preset Backups text box, and the floppy-disk or tape drive to use, which is selected using the Backup To drop-down box.

● OPTIONS: BASIC

The Basic program level gives the user access to all the options at the Preset level, plus the ability to create or change setup files (see *Setup Files* below); create and run macros (see *Macros* in the *Automating Backup* section); change file selections (see *Selecting Files* below); change the Backup type (see *Types of Backups*); and additionally, the following toggles:

Verify Backup Data compares the source file and the backed-up file. This slows the backup process but greatly improves the confidence level.

Compress Backup Data compresses the files as they are backed up, saving disk space and reducing the time needed for backup.

Prompt Before Overwriting Used Diskettes displays an alert box if you insert a diskette that has been used before. This allows you to replace the diskette with a new one or to verify that it is all right to overwrite the current one. (Not an option for tape backups.)

Password Protect Backup Sets prevents you from restoring backed-up files without a password, even when run automatically from the scheduler. (Version 2.0 only.)

Unattended Backup preforms automatic tape backups without user intervention. Prompt boxes are still displayed for 15 seconds, but if the user doesn't respond then an automatic response is used to continue the backup. (Version 2.0 and Tape Backup only.)

Retry Busy Files instructs Backup to wait for busy files before continuing the backup. This can cause substantial slowdowns on networks if backups are scheduled at busy times. (Version 2.0 and Tape Backup only.)

Generate a Backup Report generates a report on the files, options, and times of the backup, which is stored on the disk in the setup-file directory with the same name as the setup file and an extension of .RPT. (Version 2.0 and Tape Backup only.)

Display Tape Directory displays a directory of the volumes on the tape prior to beginning the backup. (Version 2.0 and Tape Backup only.)

Append Backup Data To Tape appends the current backup after any other backups on the tape. When off, Backup overwrites any other information on the tape. (Version 2.0 and Tape Backup only.)

Store Catalog On Tape stores a copy of the catalog file on the tape. This catalog is stored in a separate volume on the tape, which can cause the backup to take longer. (Version 2.0 and Tape Backup only.)

Format Tape Before Backup reformats the tape prior to backing up. This takes an additional forty minutes with QIC-40 format tapes. (Version 2.0 and Tape Backup only.)

Always Format Backup Disks always formats the backup disks, even if they are already formatted. This slows down the backups, but it also protects against disks that may have been formatted in drives whose heads were out of alignment.

Use Error Correction on Diskettes writes additional error-correction information on the diskettes to provide an additional level of data integrity. Note, however, that this error correction information will use from 11–13% of the available disk space.

Keep Old Backup Catalogs On Hard Disk keeps old back-up catalog files on the hard disk. This can be useful if you use backups to keep track of version information and you want to restore an older version of a file without having to rebuild the catalog from the disks.

Audible Prompts (Beep) beeps whenever an action is required on your part or an error condition occurs. Note that this beep will not occur if you have "Beep=no" in your WIN.INI file.

Quit After Backup automatically quits when the backup is completed.

● OPTIONS: ADVANCED

With the program level set to Advanced, all the options that are available at the Basic level remain available, with the following additions or changes:

Data Verification offers three choices for data verification:

- **Read and Compare**, which checks every byte.
- **Sample Only**, which checks every eighth track.
- **Off**, which does no checking.

Data Compression offers four choices for the level of compression:

- **Off**, which does no compression.
- **Save Time**, which does compression only while the Central Processing Unit (CPU) is idle, waiting for the floppy drive.
- **Save Space (Low)**, which tends to result in greater compression than Save Time, but runs slower on slow computers.
- **Save Space (High)**, which minimizes the amount of disk space used, but generally runs slower than the other options, except on the fastest computers.

Overwrite Warning provides several levels of overwrite warning, depending on the output device selected. For floppy disks, the options are:

- **Off**, which gives no warning before overwriting previously used diskettes.

- **DOS-Formatted Diskette**, which warns you before overwriting any DOS diskette that contains data.

- **Backup Diskettes**, which warns you before overwriting any diskette that contains Norton Backup data.

- **Any Used Diskette**, which warns you before overwriting any diskette that contains any data at all.

For tape backups (Version 2.0 only), the options are:

- **Always Append**, which places the current backup after whatever is already on the tape.

- **Always Overwrite**, which overwrites anything currently on the tape and begins from the front of the tape.

- **Overwrite On Full Backup**, which will append Differential or Incremental backups but will overwrite on a Full backup.

Unattended Backup offers five different time frames:

- **Off**, which will wait for user input at all prompts.

- **0 Second Delay**, which doesn't pause at all for user input.

- **5 Second Delay**, which pauses for five seconds at user prompts before continuing.

- **15 Second Delay**, which pauses for fifteen seconds at user prompts before continuing (the default).

- **60 Second Delay**, which waits a full minute for input before continuing.

(Version 2.0 and Tape Backup only.)

Component Size is available only when you are backing up to a DOS path. It allows you to choose the size of the backup file, which can make later transfers to diskette much easier. The options are as follows:

> **Best fit** [uses the maximum size available]
> **1.44 Mb**
> **1.2 Mb**
> **720 Kb**
> **360 Kb**

Busy File Retry Options offers several retry options on Netware 286 or 386 networks, in the case of busy files. Click on the **More>>** button to see them. They are:

- **Do Not Retry**, which will skip the file if it is busy.

- **Retry For**, which will try to back up the busy file for the period of time in hours and minutes that you enter into the text box, after which it will skip it.

- **Retry Until**, which will keep retrying busy files until the time keyed into the text box and then skip any other busy files for the rest of the backup.

- **Until Not Busy**, which will keep retrying to backup up busy files until they become free.

Report Options offers several options for tape backup when running in Advanced Mode. When any of the Include options are on, an ASCII report is saved in the directory specified for catalog files. The report will have the same name as the .SET file, but will have an .RPT extension instead. Select the **More>>** button to access these options:

- **Include Backup Options** includes the backup settings that were used for the backup.

- **Include Processed Files** includes the full filename and path of each file backed up.

- **Include Error Messages** includes all the error messages for any files that were skipped.

- **Include Backup Statistics** includes the estimated and actual time, files, and bytes backed up.

- **Append Reports** appends new reports after an existing one instead of overwriting it.

Proprietary Diskette Format uses a special diskette format that allows more data to fit on each diskette. This option may take longer and will make the diskettes uncopyable with DOS commands.

SETUP FILES

Setup files are files that you create to define a group or set of files to back up. For example, you could have a setup file that effects a total backup of your hard disk. This set would include all drives and directories on your hard disk. Another set might hold all your word-processing files, including all the files in your c:\wp51\files subdirectory. Still another might be the files required for your monthly newsletter, which could include spreadsheet, word-processing, database, and PageMaker files. Each of these might have a different backup strategy associated with it. You might do total backups only once a month with weekly incrementals, for example, but do weekly Full backups of your word-processing files, with Differential backups on a daily basis. Your newsletter, on the other hand, might get a Full backup once a month after you finish it, with nothing in between.

To Open a Setup File

1. Click **Backup, Compare,** or **Restore**.

2. Select File ➤ Open Setup. The Open Setup File dialog box will open.

3. Choose from the list of available setup files and select **OK** to open the file.

To Create a New Setup File

1. Click on the **Backup** button.

2. Click on the **Select Files** button.

3. Select the files that you want to include in this backup set. For details on selecting files, see *Selecting Files* below.

4. When you have completed your file selection, select **OK** to return to the Backup window.

5. Select the type of backup you want this to be from the **Backup Type** box.

6. Select the destination for the backup (**Backup To**).

7. Click on the **Options** button.

8. Select the options you want for this backup set.

9. Select File ➤ Save Setup As.

10. Key in the new filename for this setup file. Be sure to include the .SET extension.

To Change an Existing Setup File

1. Click the **Backup** button.

2. Open the setup file you want to modify or select it from the **Setup File** drop-down box.

3. Make the changes you want to make to the file selection, backup type, backup device, and so forth.

4. Select File ➤ Save Setup to save the changes, or select File ➤ Save Setup As to create a new setup file.

SELECTING FILES

There are many different ways to select files for backing up. The simplest way to select an individual file is to drag it from a Drive Window to the Backup icon on the desktop. For larger groups of files, though, it pays to create setup files that include all the options and files you want. See *To Create a New Setup File* for instructions on how to do so.

To Select Backup Files

1. Click on the **Backup** button to open the Backup window.

2. Click on the **Select Files** button to open the Select Backup Files window. This window, shown in Figure IV.9, has two panes—a Tree Pane and a File Pane—as well as a button bar at the bottom.

3. Select directories for backup by using one of the following methods:

- Double-click on the name of the directory in the Tree Pane to toggle the selection of its files on or off.

- Highlight the directory in the Tree Pane and then press the spacebar to toggle the selection of its files on or off.

- Highlight the directory in the Tree Pane and then press Ins to select the files in that directory or Del to deselect the files in that directory.

4. You can select individual files in the File Pane using the same methods used in step 3 for directories.

5. If you are running at the Advanced program level, you can select groups of files meeting specific criteria using the Include, Exclude, and Special buttons in the button bar at the bottom of the window.

6. Save your selections by clicking on the **OK** button or abandon them by clicking on the **Cancel** button.

● OPTIONS: BUTTON BAR

Include, which is available only at the Advanced program level, opens up the Include/Exclude Files dialog box, shown in Figure IV.10. Fill in the path for files to include in the Path text box and the file specification in the Files text box; then select the Include radio button. Check the Include Subdirectories box to include all subdirectories in the selection. Then

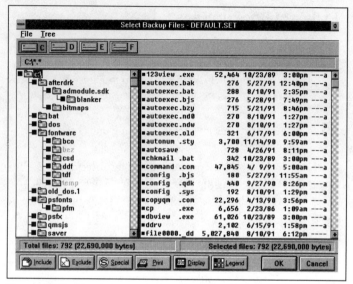

Figure IV.9: The Advanced Select Backup Files window

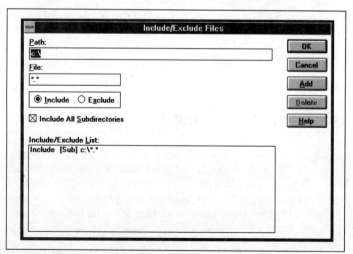

Figure IV.10: The Include/Exclude File window

click on **Add** to add this group of files to your selected files shown in the Include/Exclude list box. Highlight a description in the Include/Exclude list box and click on **Delete** to remove a group of files from the list. When you are done, choose **OK** to accept the selections or **Cancel** to abandon them.

Exclude, which is available only at the Advanced program level, also opens the Include/Exclude Files dialog box shown in Figure IV.10. Everything works the same as with Include, except that the Exclude radio button is selected. Use this to exclude groups of files.

Special, which is available only at the Advanced program level, opens the Special Selections dialog box shown in Figure IV.11. This box allows you to select files to include by a range of dates and to exclude special files such as copy-protected, hidden, system, and read-only files.

Print opens the Print File List box. This box allows you to print a list of files on the current drive or all files on your computer's drives. You cannot select individual files for inclusion on the list, and it ignores your current setup file. (All files are always printed.) You can choose to print using the graphics mode of your printer or the straight text mode, which is quicker. You can also choose to print to a file by checking the Print to File box and entering the filename in the text box. Select **OK** to print the list or **Cancel** to close the box without printing. Select the **Setup** box to open either the Printer Parameters dialog box for your printer or an information box telling you to use the Windows Control Panel, depending on the type of printer selected.

Display opens the Display Options dialog box. With this box, you can choose the amount of information to display about each file, the order in which files are displayed, whether to group selected files together, whether the Tree and File Panes are displayed side by side or top and bottom, and whether to show only certain files in the display (Filter).

Legend opens the Backup Selection Legend box. This box shows what the selection icons in the Tree and File Panes mean.

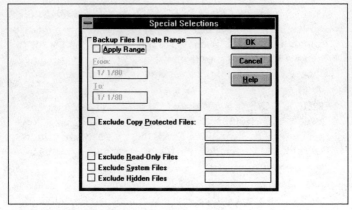

Figure IV.11: The Special Selections window

• OPTIONS: MENU

File, View opens a View window to let you view the contents of the highlighted file.

File, Delete allows you to delete the highlighted file.

File, Select All, with the cursor in the Tree Pane, selects all the files on the current drive unless specifically excluded in the Special Selections dialog box. With the cursor in the File Pane, selects all the files in the current directory unless specifically excluded in the Special Selections dialog box.

File, Deselect All deselects all the files on the current drive if in the Tree Pane or the directory if in the File Pane.

Tree, Expand One Level shows subdirectories of the highlighted directory in the Tree Pane if they are not visible, showing them one level deeper for that branch.

Tree, Expand Branch expands the display in the Tree Pane to show all subdirectories of the highlighted directory.

Tree, Expand All expands the display in the Tree Pane to show all directories on the current drive.

Tree, Collapse Branch collapses the display in the Tree Pane to show no subdirectories below the highlighted directory for that branch.

• **NOTES**   Clicking on the icon in the Tree Pane will expand or contract the tree if there are subdirectories of that directory, but it will not select files for backup. You must double-click on the directory name to toggle file selection.

If there are collapsed branches of the tree below the currently highlighted directory (as shown by a plus sign (+) in the center of the directory icon), selecting or deselecting the current directory for backup will affect its hidden directories as well. If the tree is expanded and the subdirectories are visible, then selecting or deselecting the current directory will not affect its subdirectories.

When creating a macro to automate file selection procedures, always use Ins and Del rather than the mouse or the spacebar to select files.

Both the Tree Pane and the File Pane have a feature that causes a ? to appear alongside the pointer when you move the mouse pointer to the Legend box. If you click once on the left mouse button, a message box appears:

Backup Directory Selection Information

This box gives information on the directory name, creation date, number of files in the directory, number of selected files, and the number of files to be backed up. If you are in the File Pane, it gives you information on the individual file.

THE COMPARE WINDOW

The Compare window allows you compare previously backed-up files against the files on your hard disk. Use this to verify the integrity of a backup without actually restoring the files. To reduce the time it takes to do a comparison, you can select the files to compare so that you check only irreplaceable files.

To Compare Files

1. Click on the **Configure** button to open the Configure window.

2. Select the program level to use.

3. Click on the **Compare** button to switch to the Compare window.

4. Select the backup catalog to use.

5. Select the files to compare by clicking on the **Select Files** button and selecting the files in the Select Compare Files window.

6. Select the drive from which to compare.

7. If using the Basic or Advanced program level, select the location of the files you want to compare.

8. If using the Basic or Advanced program level, click on the **Options** button to set beeps on or off and to specify whether to quit after the comparison is completed.

9. If you're using the Basic or Advanced program level and you want to use a catalog not on the default drive and directory, or you need to rebuild or retrieve a catalog, select **Catalog** from the top menu bar.

10. Click on the **Start Compare** button to begin the comparison process.

Program Levels

The same three program levels are available as in the Backup window—Preset, Basic, and Advanced—and they are set in the Configure window. Each higher step provides increased control over the details of the way Backup works.

• OPTIONS: PRESET

Backup Set Catalog contains the name and description of the master catalogs created when backup sets were made. Choose the backup set you want to compare.

Select Files opens the Select Compare Files window, where you can select the files to compare.

Compare From allows you to choose the device to use for the compare.

● OPTIONS: BASIC

The Basic and Advanced comparison options are very similar; the only difference is found in the options for selecting files. At the Basic program level, the options include all the options at the Preset level, plus the following:

Backup Set Catalog lets you choose from individual catalogs or from the master catalog from each backup set.

Compare To lets you select the location to compare the backup set with.

Options lets you choose to toggle two additional options:

- Audible Prompts (Beep)
- Quit After Compare

Catalog allows you to locate a catalog stored in another drive or directory or to rebuild or retrieve one from the backup tape or diskettes. (In Version 1.0, this is a button not a menu selection.) The options are the following:

- **Load** to load a different catalog file from a different directory.
- **Retrieve** to get a catalog file stored on the last disk of a backup set.
- **Rebuild** to rebuild a catalog file by scanning the diskettes in a backup set.
- **Delete** to delete a catalog file.

● OPTIONS: ADVANCED

The Advanced program level options are the same as in the Basic program level options, except in the Select Compare Files window, where you can select files using the Special button to include files based on a range of dates and exclude them based on file type (copy protected, read-only, system, or hidden).

To Select Files

Selecting files in the Select Compare Files window is very similar to selecting files in the Select Backup Files window. There are, however, two major differences. The first is that there is no View option available to view a file. The other is that at the Advanced program level, the Include and Exclude buttons are missing; only the Special button appears.

THE RESTORE WINDOW

Backing up files is fine, and it is a good idea to compare the backed-up files to the originals, but ultimately the reason for backing up files is so that you can restore them in the event of disaster. The restoration process is very similar to the comparison process and many of the options are the same. The main difference is that with Restore you are actually writing the files to your hard disk, not merely comparing them. Version 2.0 of Norton Backup adds an emergency restore program on the Fix-It Disk that allows you to load a limited, restore-only, non-Windows version of Norton Backup to restore files in case of a catastrophe that makes the use of Windows impossible.

To Restore Files

1. Click **Configure** to open the Configure window.
2. Select the program level to use.
3. Click **Restore** to switch to the Restore window.
4. Select the backup catalog to use.
5. Select the files to restore by clicking on the **Select Files** button and selecting the files in the Select Restore Files window.
6. Select the drive to restore from.
7. If using the Basic or Advanced program level, select the location of the files you want to restore to.
8. If using the Basic or Advanced program level, click on the **Options** button to set the options desired.

9. If you're using the Basic or Advanced program level
and you want to use a catalog not on the default drive and
directory or you need to rebuild or retrieve a catalog,
select **Catalog** from the main menu bar.

10. Click on the **Start Restore** button to begin the restore
process.

PROGRAM LEVELS

The same three program levels are available as in the Backup window—Preset, Basic, and Advanced—and they are set in the Configure window.

● OPTIONS: PRESET

Backup Set Catalog has the name and description of the
master catalogs that were created when the backup sets were
made. Choose the backup set you want to restore.

Select Files… opens the Select Restore Files window where
you can select the files to restore.

Restore From lets you choose the location from where the backed-
up files are restored.

● OPTIONS: BASIC

The Basic and Advanced restore options are very similar; the only
difference is in the options available for selecting files. At the Basic
program level, the options include all the options at the Preset level,
plus the following:

Backup Set Catalog now lets you choose from individual
catalogs or from the master catalog from each backup set.

Restore To lets you select the location to which to restore the
backup set.

Options lets you choose to toggle several additional options.
These are the following:

• **Verify Restored Files** compares the file on the
backup disk and the file written to the hard disk.

This slows the backup process but greatly improves the confidence level.

- **Prompt Before Creating Directories** asks for verification before it creates a directory.

- **Prompt Before Creating Files** asks for verification before it creates a new file that doesn't already exist on the hard disk.

- **Prompt Before Overwriting Existing Files** asks for verification before it overwrites an existing file.

- **Restore Empty Directories** creates directories that do not exist on the hard disk, even if there are no files to restore from that directory.

- **Unattended Restore** uses a set of predetermined responses to any prompts if they are unanswered in 15 seconds to continue the restore.

- **Retry Busy Files** waits for busy files when trying to restore on a Netware 286 or 386 network.

- **Generate A Restore Report** generates an ASCII report in the current catalog directory with the name *filename*.RPT where *filename* is the name of the setup file used for the restore.

- **Audible Prompts (Beep)** beeps whenever an action is required on your part or an error condition occurs. Note that this beep will not occur if you have "Beep=no" in your WIN.INI file.

- **Quit After Restore** automatically quits when the restoration is completed.

Catalog lets you locate a catalog stored in another drive or directory or rebuild or retrieve one from the backup tape or diskettes. (In Version 1.0, this is a button, not a menu option.) The options are the following:

- **Load** to load a different catalog file.

- **Retrieve** to get a catalog file stored on the last disk of a backup set.

- **Rebuild** to rebuild a catalog file by scanning the diskettes in a backup set.
- **Delete** to delete a catalog file.

• OPTIONS: ADVANCED

The Advanced program level options are similar to the Basic program level options, except in the Select Restore Files window, where you can select files using the **Special** button to include files based on a range of dates and exclude them based on file type (copy-protected, read-only, system, or hidden). The following options which are available by clicking on the **Options** button:

Data Verification offers three choices for data verification. They are:

- **Read and Compare**, which checks every byte.
- **Sample Only**, which checks every twentieth segment of a tape or every eighth track of a floppy disk.
- **Off**, which does no checking.

Overwrite Files offers three levels of overwrite protection. They are:

- **Never Overwrite** tells Backup not to restore a file if it already exists on the hard disk.
- **Older Files Only** tells Backup to restore a file to the hard disk only if the file on the hard disk is older than the file being restored.
- **Always Overwrite** tells Backup to always overwrite an existing file on the hard disk, regardless of the age of the file.

Archive Flag offers three different actions for the archive flag. They are:

- **Leave Alone**, which instructs Backup not to change the status of the archive flag when it restores the file.
- **Mark As Backed Up**, which causes Backup to set the archive flag off for all restored files.

- **Mark As NOT Backed Up**, which causes Backup to set the archive flag on for all restored files.

Busy File Retry Options offers several retry options on Netware 286 or 386 networks, in the case of busy files. Click on the **More>>** button to see them. They are:

- **Do Not Retry**, which will skip the file if it is busy.

- **Retry For**, which will try to restore the busy file for the length of time in hours and minutes that you enter into the text box, after which it will skip it.

- **Retry Until**, which will keep retrying files that are busy until the time keyed into the text box and then skip any other busy files for the rest of the restore.

- **Until Not Busy**, which will keep retrying to restore busy files until they become free.

Report Options has several report options for tape restore when running in Advanced Mode. When any of the Include options are on, an ASCII report is saved in the directory specified for catalog files. The report will have the same name as the .SET file, but will have an .RPT extension instead. Select the **More>>** button to access these options:

- **Include Restore Options** includes the restore settings that were used for the restore.

- **Include Processed Files** includes the full filename and path of each file restored.

- **Include Error Messages** includes all the error messages for any files that were skipped.

- **Include Restore Statistics** includes the estimated and actual time, files, and bytes restored.

- **Append Reports** appends new reports after an existing one, instead of overwriting the existing one.

To Select Files

Selecting files in the Select Restore Files window is the same as selecting files in the Select Compare Files window.

THE EMERGENCY RESTORE PROGRAM

Norton Backup for Windows Version 2.0 includes an Emergency
Restore progam on the Fix-It Disk. This disk contains a limited
version of the Norton Backup for DOS, which can be used to re-
restore files to your hard disk in a case where you are unable to
run Windows. Even though this is a DOS program and not a
Windows program, the look and behavior are very similar.

To Install and Use
the Emergency Restore Program

1. Place the Fix-It Disk in the A drive and type the following
at the DOS prompt

   A:Install ⏎

2. Select Color or Black and White for the display.

3. Key in the directory where you want to install the Emergency Restore program.

4. The install program will copy the files from the diskette to
the directory you selected and automatically configure the
Emergency Restore program for your hardware. Follow
the prompts as necessary.

5. Once installed and configured, you can begin the Restore
process. Select Restore from the main menu.

6. The Catalog Options window will open. Choose the
catalog option that best suits your needs.

7. Select the restore options required and then select **Start
Restore**.

● OPTIONS: CATALOG

The Emergency Restore program has three different Catalog options to choose from. They are:

   • **No Catalog**, which restores an entire backup set from disk
or tape but does not allow you to select individual files to
restore.

- **Retrieve**, which retrieves the backup catalog from the last disk or tape of a backup set and then allows you to select which files to restore.

- **Rebuild**, which recreates a backup catalog from the information on the disks or tapes and then allows you to select which files to restore.

● OPTIONS: EMERGENCY RESTORE

Once a catalog option has been selected, the Emergency Restore program offers the same options as an Advanced mode Restore from the full Windows version of the program. See *The Restore Window* for a complete listing of these options and their meanings.

AUTOMATING BACKUPS

Norton Backup provides tools for creating and using automated backups to make backing up simple and fast. Automated backups can be created only at the Basic or Advanced program level, but they can be used at any program level. You can also use the Scheduler to begin your backup automatically and run it in the background.

Setup Files

Setup files contain all that is necessary to automate a backup because they include the type of backup, the file selection, backup options, and restore and compare selections and options. You can tell Backup to use a setup file on start up by including the name of the setup file in the command line. If you want the backup to start automatically, include /a (for automatic) on the command line as well.

● EXAMPLE

To start Backup using a setup file that includes all your Quattro Pro worksheet files, select File ➤ Run in Norton Desktop for Windows and key in the following command line:

NBWIN.EXE QPRO.SET /A

Macros

Norton Backup includes a macro recorder that will record your keystrokes. You can use this, along with your setup files, to automate a complicated set of backup commands or to provide other users with the ability to select certain files while still giving them a more limited set of options.

Macros are stored with the current setup file, and only one macro can be stored with each setup file. You can record another macro even though you may have one already stored with the current setup file, but only the most recent one will be used and saved. Macros should be recorded at the level they will be used and must begin while in the Backup window, though they can be used to automate restore and compare operations as well.

If you intend to use a macro at the Preset program level, you must begin it at that level. Because there is no menu option for macros at the Preset level, you will have to use the function keys to begin, end, or insert pauses in the macro. To begin recording the macro, press **F7**. To insert a pause in the macro to allow the user to select files, press **F9**. The recording will pause until you leave the current window or dialog box and then will begin recording again. To end the macro, press **F7**.

At the Basic or Advanced program level, you can begin macros by selecting Macro ➤ Record or by pressing **F7**. To play back a macro, you must start at the Backup window, then press **F8** or select Macro ➤ Run.

You can also automatically start the macro associated with a setup file from the command line by including an @ sign in front of the setup file name on the command line.

● EXAMPLE

To automatically start the macro created to go with your Quattro Pro setup file, you would use the following command line:

NBWIN.EXE @QPRO.SET

• OPTIONS: COMMAND LINE

You can use command line options to start Backup automatically, run a specific macro and setup file, and select the type of backup. Backup supports the following command line options:

@ runs macro associated with the setup file

/A immediately starts the backup

/M runs Backup minimized

/TF does a Full Backup

/TI does an Incremental backup

/TD does a Differential backup

/TC does a Full copy backup

/TO does an Incremental copy backup

• **NOTE**   The @ and /A command line options are mutually exclusive, with the @ option overriding the /A option.

NORTON DISK DOCTOR

The Disk Doctor program runs numerous tests on your disk drives to monitor problems in the Partition Table, DOS Boot Record, File Allocation Table (FAT), and the directory and file structures. It also checks your drives for lost clusters and cross-linked files.

Disk Doctor should be used in the following situations:

- When you have trouble accessing a disk or when a disk behaves erratically.

- When files or directories seem to be missing but were not deleted.

- When you want to practice preventive maintenance to look for potential problems.

On some network configurations, you may not be able to run Disk
Doctor. You will need to exit Windows, sign off any network connections and then restart Windows. Merely disconnecting the network drive(s) inside Norton Desktop for Windows will not work.

To Use the Disk Doctor

1.   Select Tools ➤ Norton Disk Doctor or double-click on the
Disk Doctor icon in the Norton Desktop group window.

2.   Click on one or more drives in the Select Drives box.
The program starts running as soon as you click **OK**. The
name of the drive being diagnosed will appear in the title
bar. As the Disk Doctor moves through the tests, the Fill
bar tracks the progress being made for each test. If you
selected a floppy-disk drive, a window appears with
the message:

**Insert the Diskette to diagnose into Drive A: or B:
OK   Cancel**

3.   To halt the program, click on the **Pause** button, which will
then change to a Continue button. Click on the **Continue**
button to start up the program again. To stop the program,
first select **Cancel** and then select the **Exit** button.

When the tests have been completed, a list of those tests will be displayed. Select **Info** for a detailed report that can then be saved or
printed.

If an error is found, the Disk Doctor will display a message report-
ing the nature of the problem and describing the reason it should be
repaired. Problems found by the Disk Doctor can be corrected by
exiting Windows and using the Norton Disk Doctor (NDD) program included on the Fix-It Disk. See *Part Six: The Fix-It Disk
Programs.*

What the Disk Doctor Tests

Partition Table shows DOS how to find the partition(s) on
your hard disk. If the Partition Table is damaged, DOS will not
be able to access the hard disk.

Boot Record contains information about the disk's characteristics (size, layout, and so forth). If the record is corrupted, DOS cannot read the disk.

File Allocation Table (FAT) tells DOS how to find all the sectors belonging to a file. If the FAT is damaged, DOS will not be able to locate one or more files.

Directory Structure shows DOS how to find files on the disk. If the directory structure is corrupted, entire directories may be lost.

File Structure tests each file's directory entry against its FAT mapping and ensures that they agree.

Lost Clusters checks for clusters that contain valid data but that cannot be linked to a known file.

QUICK ACCESS

Quick Access is the program that provides the special group window features in Norton Desktop for Windows. To have these features available, you must use the Norton Desktop as your shell.

The basic unit of Quick Access is the group item, which can be either an application or a document and its associated application. Group items can be assigned to groups and groups can be assigned to other groups. In this way you can create a work environment that is customized specifically to your needs.

LOADING QUICK ACCESS

If you did not make Norton Desktop for Windows your Windows shell, you may want to install it now. You will save memory and increase functionality.

1. Using a text editor, open the Windows SYSTEM.INI file.

2. Change the *shell=* line to read

    shell=drive:\ndw\ndw.exe

3.   Save the file. The next time you start Windows, Norton
Desktop will be your Windows shell.

ARRANGING THE DESKTOP

The appearance of your group windows can be defined in several
ways. Group windows can display their icons in three styles, as
shown in Figure IV.12 and IV.13.

In the list style, items are arranged in a list down the window. Next
to each item is the title and any additional description.

In the icon style, the icons are arranged in rows with the title below
each icon. The icon style is the display pattern used in Windows'
Program Manager.

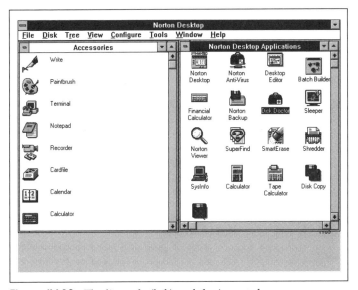

Figure IV.12: The list style (left) and the icon style

Figure IV.13: An example of the toolbox style

In the toolbox style (Version 2.0 only), group objects' icons are tiled without titles in the window. Using this style can be the most efficient use of window space.

To Choose the Group Window Display Style

1. Select Window ➤ View Group As.

2. In the View Group As dialog box, the name of the active group is shown next to Group. Select the style you want from the drop-down box. This choice will affect only the active group unless you also click the Change All Groups check box.

3. When you have made your choices, click on **OK**.

To Cascade or Tile Windows

1. Select Window ➤ Cascade (Shift-F5) *or* Window ➤ Tile (Shift-F4).

2. Tiled windows will appear as shown in Figure IV.14. An example of cascaded windows is shown in Figure IV.15.

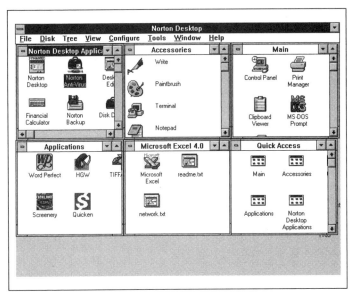

Figure IV.14: Cascaded windows

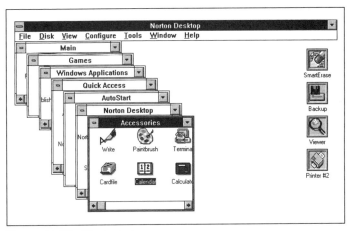

Figure IV.15: Tiled windows

To Arrange Icons

Icons can be arranged manually or automatically. You can click on an icon and drag it to its new location or you can rearrange icons by one of the following methods:

- Select Window ➤ Arrange Icons. Norton Desktop for Windows will automatically arrange the icons in the active window into neat rows.

- Select Configure ➤ Quick Access. Check the Auto Arrange Icons check box. Quick Access will arrange the icons whenever you resize the window or add an icon to the window.

CONFIGURING QUICK ACCESS

Settings for the Quick Access windows can be established through Norton Desktop's Configure menu.

To Configure Quick Access Windows

1. Select Configure ➤ Quick Access. The Configure Quick Access dialog box will open.

2. Select the style for new groups in the Create New Groups As box (Default Group View in Version 1.0). This will establish the display for new windows you create. It will not affect current windows. To change existing windows, select Window ➤ View Group As.

3. In the Settings box you can choose as follows:

    - **Auto Arrange Icons** turns on Quick Access' automatic rearrangement of icons when a window is resized or has objects added to it.

    - **Minimize on Use** causes the active window to be iconized on the desktop whenever you launch an application.

- **Name of Main Group** shows the default name for the Quick Access main group, which is Quick Access. To change the name, key in a replacement name of up to 26 characters.

- **Horizonal Spacing** and **Vertical Spacing** (Version 2.0 only) define the spacing of icons (in pixels) used when you check Auto Arrange Icons, or select Window ➤ Arrange Group Icons.

4. When you have made your choices, select the **OK** button.

● OPTIONS: CONFIGURE QUICK ACCESS

AutoStart designates an AutoStart group. Usually this will be the Windows 3.1 StartUp group or the Norton Desktop for Windows AutoStart group. Using this option, you can select any group to be the AutoStart group. All group items in the designated AutoStart group will be launched when Windows is started.

Reset Icons resets all icons to their default settings.

STARTUP

If you want one or more group items to be launched when you start Windows, you can add them to the StartUp group (AutoStart in Version 1.0). For example, you can have your desktop organizer and spreadsheet program automatically started when you begin a work session.

To Add an Item to StartUp

1. Select Window ➤ StartUp.

2. Open the window that contains the object you want to add.

3. Click and drag the object to StartUp. When you start Norton Desktop, each item in the StartUp window will launch in its own application window.

• **NOTE**   To copy an item to StartUp you must hold down **Ctrl** while clicking and dragging.

OBJECTS

Quick Access uses the term *object* to encompass both groups and group items. If you open a group, its group window opens. If you open a group item, that program will launch and open any file that is included in that group item's definition.

CREATING NEW OBJECTS

When you make a new group, it is added to the collection of groups in Quick Access. When you make a subgroup, it is added to the active group. A new group item is added to whatever group is active when the group item is created.

To Create a New Group

1. To create a subgroup in an existing group, open the existing group and click on it to make it active. To make a top level group, make the Quick Access main group active.

2. Select File ➤ New.

3. Select the Group radio button in the Type box.

4. In the Title text box, key in the name you want to appear on the title bar of the new group. This name will also appear under its icon in the Quick Access window.

5. Key in a Group File Name if desired. Click on the Browse button to search through the drives and files for existing group filenames. (Version 1.0: You can include a description and a shortcut key here if you want to.)

6. The current icon for the group is shown at the top of the dialog box. To select a different icon, click on the Icon button. (See *To Change an Object's Icon* later in this section.)

7. Click on the **Options** button (Version 2.0 only) to select a startup directory, description, and shortcut key. Click the **Password** button to assign a password and to restrict access to the group. (See *To Maintain a Password* later in this section.) Other options in this dialog box apply when creating a group item. See *To Create a New Group Item* below.

8. Click on **OK** when finished.

To Create a New Group Item Using the Mouse

1. Open a Drive Window for the drive with the program or file you want. Use the directory tree and File Panes to locate the file.

2. Open the group window that is to be the new object's destination.

3. Click on the program or file name and drag it to its destination window. The icon for that program or document will now appear in the group window.

To Create a New Group Item

1. Select the group where you want the item assigned.

2. Select File ➤ New.

3. In the Type box, select **Item**. The object will become a group item icon in the active window.

4. In the Title text box, key in the object's title. The title will appear under the object's icon in the window (if you are using the icon-display style) or next to the icon (if you are using the list-display style). You can also leave this blank and Quick Access will assign a title using either the application name or the document name (for a document associated with an application).

5. In the Group File Name text box (Program/Document/Script in Version 1.0), key in the name of the file you want executed when this group item is opened. If you

156 Tools and Utilities

also want to open a particular document with the program, press the spacebar once and then key in the document filename.

6. To change the default icon, click on the **Icon** button. (See *To Change an Object's Icon* below).

7. Click on the **Options** button (Version 2.0 only) for the next steps. In the Startup Directory, key in the path for the directory that Quick Access is to switch to when this object is open. If you do not include this information, your program may not be able to find all the files it needs to run.

8. Key in a description and specify shortcut keys if you want them.

9. Select the **Password** button to set a Password. (See *To Maintain a Password* later in this section).

10. Click on **OK** when finished.

● **NOTE** In the Group File Name (Program/Document/Script) text box you do not need to include the full directory path for the application if the path is part of your AUTOEXEC.BAT file or the application is in one of the following directories:

- The Windows directory
- The Windows System directory
- The current directory

CHANGING OBJECTS

All the properties of an object, its directory path, icon, title, shortcut keys, and so forth can be changed at any time after the object's creation.

To Change an Object's Icon

1. For an existing object, select the object by clicking on it once. Choose File ➤ Properties. Click on the **Icon** button.

2.   For a new object, select the **Icon** button in the New dialog
box, as described in *To Create a New Group* or *To Create a
New Group Item* earlier in this section.

3.   The Choose Icon dialog box opens.

4.   Use the scroll bar under the Icon(s) box to see the icons
available in the current file. (Version 1.0: Click on the
prompt button for the Icon(s) drop-down box.) If you
want to use one of the icons shown, click on it.

5.   If you want to see the icons in a different file, click on the
prompt button for the Alternate Icon File box (Version 1.0:
Key in the name of library file and click on the **View** button.)

or

Click on the **Browse** button to open the Select an Icon
source-file dialog box. Highlight a file and double-click on
it to return the file and its path to the Alternate Icon File
text box. (Version 1.0: Click on the **View** button.)

6.   Highlight the icon you want in the Icon(s) box and click
on **OK**. Click on **OK** again in the Properties box to confirm
your choices.

To create your own icon, or to edit an existing one, choose Tools ➤
Icon Editor. (See *Icon Editor* above.)

● **SHORTCUT**   A more direct route to the Choose Icon dialog
box is to drag an icon from its group window to the desktop and, by
clicking once, to open the icon's control menu. Select **Icon** from the
Control menu. (See *To Turn on the Drive/Tool Icon* in *Configuring the
Desktop*.)

To Maintain a Password

1.   For a new item, select **Password** in the New dialog box.

2.   For an existing item, select **Password** from the Properties
dialog box.

3. In the Password text box, key in any combination of letters and numbers up to twenty characters long. The password appears as a series of asterisks to keep anyone from seeing it as you key it in. Click on **OK**.

4. You will be asked to confirm the password by keying it in again. After you key in the password a second time, press **Enter** or select **OK**. If the second password entry does not match the first, no password will be set.

● **NOTE** Be sure to save your password using Configure ➤ Save Configuration or by turning on the Save Configuration on Exit check box in the Preferences dialog box (Configure ➤ Preferences). If you do not save your password, it will be in effect for the current session of Quick Access only.

To Disable a Password

1. If an object is password-protected, you will need to provide the password in order to open the Properties dialog box.

2. In the Properties dialog box, select **Password**.

3. Key in the current password and press **Enter** or click **OK**.

4. When prompted for the new password, select **OK** or press **Enter**. Repeat this procedure in the Confirm Disable Current Password dialog box. Select **OK** in the Properties box to confirm the change.

To Change an Object's Properties

1. Select the **object**.

2. Select File ➤ Properties.

3. The Properties dialog box will open. Except for its title, this box is identical to the New dialog box described in *To Create a New Group* and *To Create a New Group Item* earlier in this section.

4. Change existing properties or add new ones. Select **OK** when finished.

- **NOTE** Properties that cannot be changed will appear dimmed in the Properties box. You cannot change any properties of the Quick Access main group except its title. (See *Configure Quick Access*, above.)

To Delete an Object

1. Select the **object** to be deleted.

2. Select File ➤ Delete.

3. A warning box appears asking you to confirm the deletion. If you are deleting a group, the warning box advises you that the group and all its items and subgroups will also be deleted.

4. Verify your selection and click on **Yes** to carry out the deletion.

- **SHORTCUT** You can also delete an object by highlighting it and pressing **Del**.

- **NOTE** Deleting a program or document from the desktop or from a group does not delete the files from your disk. The icon will be removed, but the underlying files will remain.

To Move or Copy an Object Using the Mouse

1. Open both the object's current window and the window to receive it.

2. To move the object, click and drag it from its current window to the new window. To copy the object, hold down **Ctrl** while dragging the object.

To Move or Copy an Object Using the Keyboard

1. Select File ➤ Move or File ➤ Copy.

2. In the From box, highlight the item you want to move or copy.

3. In the To box, highlight the destination group.

4. Click on **OK** when finished or **Cancel** to abandon the operation.

OPENING OBJECTS

There are four ways to open a group window and three ways to open a group item.

To Open a Group Window

Do *one* of the following procedures:

- Select the group icon and press **Enter**.
- Double-click on the group icon.
- Select the icon, then choose File ➤ Open.
- Select the group from the list in the Window menu. If more than seven windows are available, click on **More** to see the entire list in a scroll-box window. Choose the group from the list and open it either by double-clicking on its name or by highlighting its name and selecting **OK**.

To Open a Group Item

Do *one* of the following procedures:

- Select the group item icon and press **Enter**.
- Double-click on the group item icon.
- Select the icon and choose File ➤ Open.

SCHEDULER

The Scheduler allows you to run programs and display messages at preset times, organizing these tasks on an events list. For example, when you first install Norton Desktop for Windows, you are asked if you want to run an automatic backup of files at 4:00 p.m. every day. If you answer Yes, the Scheduler starts up with a Daily Backup ready to run. (You still have to configure Norton Backup for the actual procedure.)

To Add an Event to Scheduler

1. Select Tools ➤ Scheduler or double-click on the Scheduler icon in the Norton Desktop group window.

2. Click on the **Add** button to see the Add Event window, shown in Figure IV.16.

3. Key in a description of the event in the Description box. This is the text that will appear on the events list.

4. Select **Run Program** or **Display Message**. Key in the command line to execute or the message to display.

5. Set the time and date for the event to take place. When finished, click **OK**.

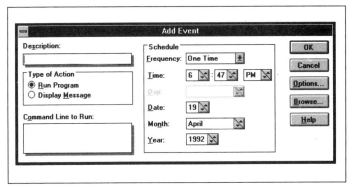

Figure IV.16: The Add Event window in Scheduler

162   Tools and Utilities

• OPTIONS: SCHEDULER

Hide When Iconized causes the icon to be hidden
when Scheduler is minimized but still active. To reopen
the Scheduler, select Tools ➤ Scheduler or double-click on
the **Scheduler** icon in the Norton Desktop window.

Load With Windows modifies the Windows WIN.INI file to
automatically load Scheduler when Windows starts. Check this
box if you have any events scheduled for daily, weekly, or
monthly intervals.

• OPTIONS: SCHEDULER ADD WINDOW

Run Program tells Scheduler to launch a Windows program,
non-Windows program, DOS command, or batch file.

Command Line to Run allows you to enter a command line
of up to 128 characters or select your program by using the
Browse button. The Scheduler will launch any executable file
or any file with an extension associated with an application.
(See *Part Two, Associating a File Extension with a Program*.)

Run Minimized (Version 1.0 only) causes the scheduled program to run minimized rather than full screen.

Display Message displays a message at a scheduled time. Enter
the message in the Message to Display box. At the prescribed date
and time, the message will appear on your screen and a beep will
sound. The message remains on the screen until you click on **OK**.

Schedule Frequency allows you to schedule events and messages in the following interval categories: one time, hourly,
weekdays, weekly, or monthly. The various scheduling boxes
activate or dim-out, depending on the category chosen.

Options (Version 2.0 only) lets you key in the start-up directory for the program file to be launched. Select the Run Style:
Normal, Minimized, or Maximized.

To Edit, Copy, or Remove Events

1. Open the Scheduler and use the mouse to highlight an event.

2. Click on **Edit** to modify the details of an event. Click on **Copy** to place a copy of the event on the main list. Click on **Delete** to delete the event from the list.

● **NOTES**   The Scheduler must be active for messages to appear or for programs to be launched. Turn on the Load With Windows box in the Scheduler for the program to be loaded automatically when Windows starts.

Events will not be launched while you have the Add Event or Edit Event window open in Scheduler. Until you finish and minimize the window, Scheduler will be disabled.

You can change the display of dates and times by altering the International settings in the Windows Control Panel.

SCREEN SAVER

The Screen Saver (Sleeper in Version 1.0) is a screen-saver package that protects your monitor screen from "burn in" by displaying a constantly moving image when you are not actively using the mouse or keyboard. Screen Saver also includes password protection to prevent anyone from clearing the screen saver and accessing the screen. In Version 2.0, Screen Saver has the added the ability to automatically use screen-saver images from other packages, such as Intermission, After Dark Version 1 (but not Version 2), and the Windows 3.1 screen saver.

Choosing a Screen-Saver Graphic

1. Choose Tools ➤ Screen Saver or double-click on the Screen Saver icon in the Norton Desktop group window.

2. Click on the Enable check box in the lower-right corner of the Screen Saver dialog box to activate the program. The default for Enable is "on."

3. Select a graphic from the scrolling box on the left side of the screen. When you click on a choice, a description and configuration choices, if any, will appear in the center box.

4. Click on the **Sample** button to see a display of the image you chose. Use the scroll bars and check boxes in the sample window to adjust the image.

5. Select the **Restore** button to return to the main Screen Saver dialog box.

● OPTIONS: CHECK BOXES

Hide When Iconized causes the Screen Saver icon to disappear. The program will remain active but to review or change Screen Saver options you must choose Tools ➤ Screen Saver or double-click on the Screen Saver icon in the Norton Desktop group window.

Load With Windows changes the Windows WIN.INI file to load the Screen Saver program whenever Windows is started.

Enable turns the Screen Saver program on and off.

● OPTIONS: PREFERENCES

Time Trigger Boxes causes the screen-saver graphic to appear after a set period of time without input from the keyboard or mouse. The default setting is five minutes, but you can set it to appear at any interval from ten seconds to 999 minutes and 59 seconds.

Sleep Now Corner selects a corner that will activate the Screen Saver function almost immediately when the mouse pointer is parked there.

Sleep Never Corner overrides the time set in the Time Trigger boxes when you move the mouse pointer to the selected corner, preventing the screen-saver graphic from appearing.

Use Sleep Corners turns the Sleep Corners on and off.

Use Sleep Hot Keys enables the use of keyboard hot keys to turn the screen-saver graphic on.

Select Hot Keys places the cursor in the text box; select a single key or two keys in combination to act as an immediate activator of the screen-saver graphic. Your choice of Hot Key(s) will appear on the main Screen Saver dialog box in the lower-left corner. If the Use Sleep Hot Keys check box is not selected, the entry in the Select Hot Keys text box will be dimmed-out and the Hot Key on the main Screen Saver dialog box will show as Disabled.

● **NOTE**   Choose hot keys carefully. If you pick a combination that duplicates a key combination in Norton Desktop for Windows or Windows, you may cause a conflict in your system.

● OPTIONS: PASSWORD

No Password requires no password; this is the default setting.

Use Network Password requires the network password, if you have one, to wake up the screen.

Custom Password allows you to choose a password that will be required to wake up the screen. Key in the password and click on **OK**. Asterisks will appear in the box to prevent anyone from looking over your shoulder and seeing your password, so a second box asks you to enter the password again.

● **NOTE**   The password protects only the screen that you were looking at before the screen saver activated. It does not protect your system files, which can be accessed simply by rebooting.

● OPTIONS: WAKE UP

Wake On Key Strokes wakes up the screen when any key is pressed.

Wake On Mouse Clicks causes the screen to reappear when a mouse button is clicked.

Wake On Mouse Movement causes the screen-saver graphic to disappear when the mouse is moved.

• **NOTE** Screen Saver must be active in order to run. You can load it by selecting it from the Tools menu and then clicking on the Minimize box. A more convenient way is to click on the Load With Windows option described above. If you close the Screen Saver, it becomes inactive.

SHREDDER

Shredded files are deleted permanently from your system. Unlike files removed with the Delete command, they cannot be retrieved using UnErase. By default, the Shredder overwrites the selected file with zeroes.

To Shred a File or Subdirectory

1. To bring up the Shredder dialog box, do one of the following:

   • Double-click on the Shredder icon on the desktop.

   • Double-click on the Shredder icon in the Norton Desktop group window.

   • Select Tools ➤ Shredder.

2. Key in the name of the file or directory to be shredded. If you are not sure of the location of the file you want to shred, click on the **Browse** button to scan drives and directories for file names. Click on Include Subdirectories to shred files in subdirectories and the subdirectories themselves.

3. Click on **OK**. A warning box will pop up twice for each file and subdirectory with the reminder that shredding a file is permanent. If you want to proceed, click on **Yes** in each warning box.

• **SHORTCUT** Click on a file name in a Drive Window and drag the file's icon to the Shredder icon on the desktop.

● **WARNING!**   *Be careful not to shred more files than you intend. Shredded files are destroyed permanently and cannot be recovered by any normal means.*

● **NOTES**   To designate a shredding pattern other than the default, select Configure ➤ Shredder and pick a pattern from the following:

US Government Shredding overwrites the file with a government standard shred that uses decimal character 246 as the last character. This method overwrites the file repeatedly and is significantly slower than the normal default method, which overwrites using zeroes.

Use Special Over-Write Pattern allows you to specify a decimal value from 0 to 255 to use as a file overwrite pattern. The use of a special pattern does not slow the shredding process.

Repeat Count specifies the number of times the file will be overwritten.

Sophisticated data recovery devices *may* be able to recover data unless you have used the US Government Shredding method. Normal means, such as using UnErase or other data recovery utilities, will not be able to recover shredded files regardless of the shredding method chosen.

SMARTERASE AND UNERASE

Using the SmartErase and UnErase utilities, you can provide many levels of protection for your files. With SmartErase enabled, you can be sure of being able to recover all deleted files within the limits of parameters you set. Files that have been marked for protection are saved by SmartErase in a hidden directory called *Trashcan*. Recovery of files from the Trashcan directory is both swift and certain.

In order for SmartErase to be enabled, you must have the line

SMARTCAN /ON /SKIPHIGH

in your AUTOEXEC.BAT file (**ep /on** in Version 1.0). Norton
Desktop for Windows will add the line to your AUTOEXEC.BAT at
the time of installation if you choose. Even without SmartErase,
you can usually recover deleted files using UnErase alone,
provided you act promptly. UnErase is always enabled, but file
recovery is not guaranteed.

To Recover a File Using SmartErase

1. Select Tools ➤ UnErase or double-click on the SmartErase
   icon on the desktop. The SmartErase dialog box opens, as
   shown in Figure IV.17.

2. Click on the directory or subdirectory in the left pane for
   the file you want to recover. Deleted files will be listed
   in the right pane. Files with the first character changed to
   a question mark are unprotected files deleted by DOS.
   These files may be recoverable if unerased promptly.

3. Select the file you want to recover and click on the **Un-
   Erase** button. The file will be recovered, removed from the
   UnErase window and restored to its original position.

4. If the file is one that was deleted while unprotected, you
   will see a new dialog box with the message

   **DOS has overwritten the first letter of the filename.
   Please provide a new first letter.**

   Enter a new first letter for the filename and select **OK**. The
   file has now been recovered. If the file is not recoverable,
   you will see an error message.

• OPTIONS: SMART ERASE/UNERASE

Purge removes designated files from the SmartErase window
and from the Trashcan directory. Files that are purged are no
longer protected by SmartErase.

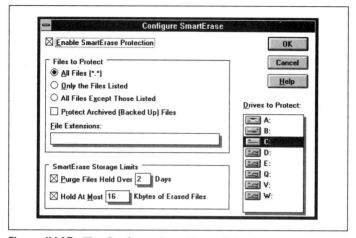

Figure IV.17: The Configure SmartErase dialog box

Hide Old/Show Old toggles the display to show or hide old files, including duplicate entries and entries that were deleted long ago.

● **SHORTCUT**   Use the Tab key to highlight the directory or file window and begin keying in the name of the directory or file you want. The highlight cursor will move to the first entry that matches your keystrokes.

To Configure SmartErase

To conserve disk space, you may not want to have SmartErase preserve every file that has been deleted, or you may want to limit the time that SmartErase protects deleted files.

1. Select Configure ➤ SmartErase.

2. Select the drives you wish to protect. From the options offered, enter the parameters for the files you wish protected and choose the storage limits you want.

3. Click on **OK** to accept your choices or **Cancel** to abandon the operation.

• OPTIONS: SMARTERASE

If the **Enable SmartErase Protection** line is dimmed-out, it means that the erase protection program is not installed in your AUTOEXEC.BAT. If the box is checked, it can be selected and cleared to disable SmartErase.

Drives and Files to Protect

Click on the drives you want to protect. SmartErase will create a Smartcan directory on each protected drive (Trashcan in Version 1.0). The default is all local hard drives on your system.

All files protects all files on the drives selected.

Only the files listed protects only certain types of files; you can list up to nine file extensions in the File Extensions text box. These extensions must be separated from each other by a space or comma.

All files except those listed protects all files except those whose extensions are listed in the File Extensions text box.

Protect archived (backed up) files protects files that have not been changed since their last backup. The default is off because it is presumed that these files, if accidentally deleted, could be recovered from backup disks.

• OPTIONS: SMARTERASE STORAGE LIMITS

You can select either a storage time limit or a size limit or both.

For **Time**, select the Purge Files Held Over X Days check box. Enter the number of days that you want the files protected. The possible range is from one day to 99. If this box is selected without also selecting the Size box, the Smartcan directory may become very large, taking up too much space on your hard disk.

For **Size**, fill in the amount of disk space that you want allotted to protected files in the line Hold at Most X Kbytes of Erased Files. If you choose this check box, the minimum size you can set for the Smartcan directory is 16K and the maximum size is 9,999K. When the size limit is reached, SmartErase will purge the oldest files from the Smartcan.

SYSTEM INFO

System Information displays and prints detailed reports of your computer's hardware and software characteristics, including benchmark comparisons of your system with other popular computers.

To Use System Information

1.   Choose Tools ➤ System Info or double-click on its icon in the Norton Desktop group window.

2.   The System Summary window is displayed, as shown in Figure IV.18. Click the buttons at the top of the window for the reports you want to see or select from the reports in the Summary menu.

3.   To print one or more reports, choose File ➤ Report Options. Use the mouse to select the reports you want to print. Click on **OK**. Then choose File ➤ Print Report.

4.   To save a report, choose File ➤ Save Report. In the Save Report dialog box, you may select a directory by scrolling in the directory tree box. Double-click on your choice. Key in a file name in the File text box and click on **OK** to save the file.

• OPTIONS: SYSTEM REPORTS

System Summary provides detailed information about your systems's hardware and configuration, including network information if appropriate.

Disk Summary initially displays a summary of all the hard drives. Click anywhere on a summary line to bring up a detailed Drive Window with information on the characteristics of the drive, such as the number of sectors, sectors per cluster, and so forth. When you select this report, a Window menu is added to the menu bar so you can arrange and select the Drive Windows.

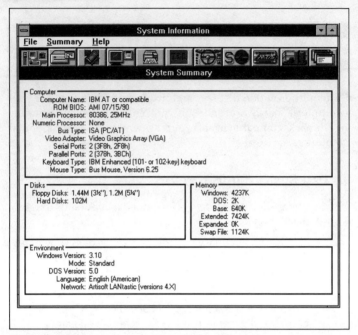

Figure IV.18: The System Summary window

Windows Memory displays a graphical representation of the memory both used and unused in Windows.

Display Summary reports video type, technology, and capabilities. Use scroll bars to access the entire listing.

Printer Summary describes the characteristics and capabilities of your printer. If more than one printer is installed, the information is provided only for the one designated as active.

TSR Summary lists the terminate-and-stay-resident (TSR) programs in memory. Includes information about size and addresses.

DOS Device Driver Summary shows the address, name, and description of the device drivers in memory.

Real Mode Software Interrupts stores addresses and owners of software interrupts. A complete understanding of interrupts is useful for diagnosing and correcting hardware and software conflicts.

CMOS Summary reports on the information contained in the battery-powered CMOS chip. This chip maintains data on the drives and memory that the computer needs when booting up.

Processor Benchmark tests the speed of your computer's central processor (CPU) and shows a bar chart comparing it to other popular computers.

Startup Files opens a pane for each of your startup files: AUTOEXEC.BAT, CONFIG.SYS, WIN.INI, SYSTEM.INI, and NDW.INI. A Window menu is added to the menu bar so you can switch between the panes and rearrange them; an Edit! item is added to the menu bar as well. Click on this to open the Desktop Editor with all of these files open for editing.

Part Five

The Norton Windows Batch Language

Under DOS, batch files make it easier to do everyday operations. They are simple ASCII text files (with .BAT extensions) that have each command on a separate line. With a simple keystroke, batch files perform a series of commands automatically, relieving the user of the burden of remembering all of them.

The Norton Windows Batch Language provides this capability, and much more, for the Windows environment. Windows Batch Language files are simple ASCII text files (with the .WBT extension) that contain commands to perform Windows operations automatically. They can be edited with any editor or word processor that can produce ASCII output or with Batch Builder. Batch Builder, which in Version 2.0 is derived from the Norton Desktop Editor, has two important advantages over other editors for editing of .WBT files. The first is that it has a handy built-in, online reference to the Windows Batch Language commands. You can select the command you want from this reference and paste it straight into your Windows batch file. The second advantage, new in Version 2.0, is its ability to run batch files in the editor for testing and debugging. The Windows Batch Language can help you to create interactive, intelligent scripts to automate many ordinary tasks in Windows.

There are several points to keep in mind when writing Windows Batch Language files. Like regular DOS batch files, each command must be on a separate line. Further, the entire command must be on one line. Due to this book's space limitations, many of the examples below wrap onto a second line; but when you write your own Windows Batch Language files, *don't* break commands in the middle of the line. Also, any line that begins with a semicolon is ignored by the Windows Batch Runner program, which runs batch files. You can take advantage of this feature to add comments to batch files to make them easier to understand and maintain.

For information on Desktop Editor and Batch Builder, see *Part 4, Desktop Editor*.

A comprehensive listing of the Norton Windows Batch commands follows, along with their syntax and an example.

● **NOTE** Not all examples are functional on a standalone basis.

Abs(integer)   Returns the positive (absolute) value of an integer. **Example:**
   delta = Abs(i–j)

AskLine(title,prompt,default)   Requests a line of data from the user. The entire response is returned if the user clicks on **OK** or presses **Enter**. **Cancel** aborts processing of the batch file. **Example:**

   User = AskLine("UserName", "Please Enter Your Name:", "")

AskPassword("Title", "Prompt")   Requests a password from the user, which it displays as "*" characters. (Version 2.0) **Example:**

   pword = AskPassword("Access Restricted", "Please Enter Your Password")

AskYesNo(title,question)   Requests a Yes, No, or Cancelresponse from the user, returning @YES or @NO. **Cancel** aborts processing of the batch file. **Example:**

   rep = AskYesNo("BackupTime?", "ready to backup your work?")

Average(integer(, integer)…)   Yields the integer average of a series of integers, separated by commas. Because the result is an integer, substantial rounding error is possible. **Example:**

   TomAge = 25
   DickAge = 30
   HarryAge = 35
   AvgAge = Average(TomAge, DickAge, HarryAge)
   Message("The average age of Tom, Dick, and Harry is: ", AvgAge)

Beep   Produces a single, short beep. This beep will not be heard, however, if your WIN.INI file contains the line "Beep=no". **Example:**

   Beep
   AskYesNo("DATA ALERT!!!", "This could permanently destroy data. Are you SURE you want to proceed?")

178 The Norton Windows Batch Language

Call(filename.wbt,parameters)   Passes control to another
.WBT file temporarily. It can also pass parameters to the secondary .WBT file. All variables are global to both the main .WBT file
and the secondary one and can be modified by the secondary file.
Multiple parameters are separated by spaces. If parameters are
passed, they will automatically be converted to "param1",
"param2", and so forth. The variable "param0" will contain the
number of parameters passed. The secondary file should end with
a "Return" statement to pass control back to the main file. **Example:**

> **Call("qprobak.wbt", "*.wq1 *.wq!")**

CallExt(filename.wbt,parameters)   Calls a secondary .WBT
file in a similar fashion to Call, except that CallExt variables are *local* to
each file (as opposed to global). Parameters can still be passed to the
secondary file. If multiple parameters are passed, they will be converted to "param1", "param2", and so forth, automatically. The variable "param0" will contain the number of parameters passed. A
"Return" statement is required at the end of the secondary file to
return control to the calling file. **Example:**

> **CallExt("savefile.wbt",currentfile)**

Char2Num(string)   Takes a text string and converts its first
character to its ANSI code equivalent. The returned value is an integer. **Example:**

> **strvar = "Alex"**
>
> **ansi = Char2Num(strvar)**
>
> **Message("ANSI Eq", "The ANSI equivalent of the first
> character in %strvar% is: %ansi%")**

ClipAppend(string)   Adds a string to the Windows Clipboard
at the end of its contents. The Clipboard must either be empty or
contain only text data, otherwise an error message will be returned.
If the append is successful, the function returns @TRUE; if it is un-
successful, it returns @FALSE. **Example:**

> **response = AskLine("UserName", "What is your name?",
> "")**
>
> **ClipAppend(response)**

ClipGet( )   Gets the current contents of the Windows Clipboard and returns it as a single string. The Clipboard must contain only text. **Example:**

> ;The following will get the user's name, convert it
> ;to uppercase, and store it in the variable "Name".
> response = AskLine("UserName", "What is your name?", "")
> ClipPut(StrUpper(response))
> Name = ClipGet()
> Message("Name Returned", Name)

ClipPut(string)   Copies a string to the Windows Clipboard. Unlike ClipAppend, it *replaces* the contents of the Clipboard.

DateTime()   Returns the date and time of the system as a formatted string. The format may be altered by changing the international section of the WIN.INI file. This can be changed either by editing it directly or by using the International section of the Control Panel. **Example:**

> Message("The current date and time are: ", DateTime())

Debug(@ON ¦ @OFF)   Toggles debug mode on or off. When debug mode is @ON, WinBatch will step through the .WBT file, displaying a dialog box with the statement just executed, any results from that statement, the errors from that step, and the next statement to execute. When debug mode is @OFF, the default, batch files execute normally. **Example:**

> ;This next runs the batch file step by step
> Debug(@ON)

Delay(seconds)   Inserts a pause in the batch file of from 2–15 seconds. **Example:**

> Message("!!WAIT!!", "Please be patient, this may take a while")
> Delay(5)
> Message("Done", "OK, that is done now.")

DialogBox("title", "filename.wbd")   Pops up a Windows dialog box. The contents and appearance of this dialog box are controlled by a template file. This template file must have the extension .WBD.

Each item in a .WBD file is enclosed in brackets ([]) and contains a variable plus one of the following symbols:

Symbol	Meaning
+	check box
#	text box
\	file selection list box
^	Option button
$	Variable

The check-box and option-button symbols each require a number representing a value that gets assigned to the variable when the box or button is selected. Following the number is the text that will appear beside the button or box. Anything not within square brackets is displayed as text. The first item that appears in a group of option buttons will always be the default. Note that template files are limited to 15 lines and the first 60 columns and may not contain tab characters. **Example:**

>   **DialogBox("Edit a File", "ed_diag.wbd")**

DirChange((d:)path)   Changes to a new directory and optionally to a new drive. Returns @TRUE if the change was successful, @FALSE if not. **Example:**

>   **DirChange("c:\")**
>   **TextBox("The contents of your autoexec.bat file", "autoexec.bat")**

DirGet()   Returns a string whose value is the path of the current directory. Useful when you want to change directories temporarily, but be sure to return to the original directory when finished. **Example:**

>   **startpoint = DirGet()**

```
DirChange("c:\")
TextBox("The contents of your autoexec.bat file are:",
"autoexec.bat")
DirChange(startpoint)
```

DirHome()   Returns a string whose value is the drive and directory of the WINBATCH.EXE file. **Example:**

```
homedir = DirHome()
Message("The WinBatch executable files are in
",homedir)
```

DirItemize(dirlist)   Returns a list of directories, separated by spaces. Used with ItemSelect, which requires a list separated by spaces. Accepts wildcards in its arguments. **Example:**

```
diravail = DirItemize("*")
```

DirMake((d:)path)   Makes a new subdirectory. Returns @TRUE if successful, @FALSE if not. **Example:**

```
DirMake("\winstuff")
```

DirRemove(dirlist)   Deletes one or more directories. Accepts a list of directories separated by spaces. Does not allow wildcards. Returns @TRUE if successful, @FALSE if not. **Example:**

```
DirRemove("temp" "junk" "\garbage")
```

DirRename((d:)oldpath, (d:)newpath)   Changes the name of a directory. Returns @TRUE if successful, @FALSE if not. **Example:**

```
DirRename("\ndwtemp", "\ndwicons")
```

DirWindows(flag)   Returns a string whose value is the Windows drive and directory if flag = 0 or the Windows system directory if flag = 1. (Version 2.0) **Example:**

```
winhome = DirWindows(0)
Message("WinInfo", "The Windows directory is
%winhome%.")
```

DiskFree(drivelist)   Returns the total of free disk space on one or more drives. Accepts a list of drives, separated by spaces. Ignores all except the first character of each item in the list, so it treats "c:\ d:\win" the same as "c d". **Example:**

> dfree = DiskFree("d")
>
> Message("D: Drive", "There are %dfree% bytes of space free on D:")

DiskScan(flag) Returns a string whose value is a list of drives, separated by spaces (e.g., "A: B: C:"). If the flag is = 0, it returns a list of unused disk drives, if flag = 1 it returns a list of floppy drives, if flag = 2 it returns a list of local hard drives, and if flag = 4, it returns a list of network drives. The values for flag are *additive* (e.g., the 3 flag is the 1 flag *and* the 2 flag). (Version 2.0) **Example:**

> drives = DiskScan(3)
>
> Message("Local Drives", "This computer has drives %drives% present locally.")

Display(seconds, window title, message) Displays a text message box. Unlike Pause, Display may be canceled with any keystroke or mouse click. **Example:**

> Display(5,"Coffee Time", "Please be patient, this may take a while")

DOSVersion(@MAJOR ! @MINOR) Returns the current DOS version number, either the major or minor revision number. **Example:**

> main = DOSVersion(@MAJOR)
>
> rev = DOSVersion(@MINOR)
>
> Display(5,"DOS Revision", "This computer is using DOS Version %main%.%rev%.")

Drop(var (, var)…) Eliminates a variable and its name, freeing up the memory associated with it. **Example:**

> foo = "A silly long string that takes up a lot of space and memory, but doesn't do anything useful."
>
> Drop(foo) ; Frees up the memory and space used by foo.

EndSession( ) This quits Windows and exits to DOS. It will save any configuration changes you may have made *if* NDW.INI has

SAVE=TRUE in its configuration section. If not, any changes will be abandoned. **Example:**

> **done = AskYesNo ("End Session?", "Are you sure you want to Quit?")**
>
> **If done == @YES Then Goto quit**
>
> **Display(3,"", "End Session Aborted")**
>
> **Exit**
>
> **:quit**
>
> **EndSession()**

Environment(variable)   Queries the DOS environment for a specific variable and returns the value of that variable as a string. **Example:**

> **dosprompt = Environment("PROMPT")**
>
> **Display(3,"Prompt", "The current DOS Prompt is: %dosprompt%")**

ErrorMode(@CANCEL ¦ @NOTIFY ¦ @OFF)   Modifies the effect of an error in a batch file. The default is @CANCEL, which cancels the execution of the batch file. @NOTIFY causes the error to be reported to the user, who can choose to continue if the error is not a fatal one. @OFF causes minor errors to be suppressed. Moderate to fatal errors are reported to the user, who can elect to continue if it isn't a fatal error. Returns the previous mode. **Example:**

> **; The Following will delete the file "temp.jnk" from the**
>
> **; c:\garbage directory, if it exists, but if it doesn't, it**
>
> **; will not cause an error message, but will continue to the**
>
> **; next line of the batch file.**
>
> **prevmode = ErrorMode(@OFF)**
>
> **FileDelete ("c:\garbage\temp.jnk")**
>
> **ErrorMode(prevmode)**

Exclusive(@OFF ¦ @ON)   This is a toggle that determines whether other Windows programs get a share of the processing time. Defaults to @OFF, which doesn't interfere with other programs, but will tend to run somewhat slower if there are several windows open.

When set to @ON it will prevent other Windows programs from getting any processing time. Returns the previous mode. **Example:**

    prevmode = Exclusive(@ON)

Execute (statement)   Allows you to execute a batch statement in a protected environment. If an error occurs, you can recover from it. This is ideal for letting users execute a statement without risking an abort of the batch file. **Example:**

    usercmd = ""
    usercmd = AskLine("Batch Executer", "What batch file
    would you like to execute?",usercmd)
    Execute Call(usercmd,"")

Exit   Causes the batch file to stop executing. Used to quit a batch file without processing it all the way to the end.

FileAppend(sourcelist, destination)   Copies one or more source files onto the end of the destination file. **Example:**

    FileAppend("*.bat", "batch.lst")

FileAttrGet("filename")   Returns a string whose value is the file's attributes. (Version 2.0) **Example:**

    filename = "C:\MSDOS.SYS"
    attribute = FileAttrGet(filename)
    Message("System File", "The attribute of %filename% is
    %attribute%.")
    ; Returns "R-SH" for this file

FileAttrSet("filespec", "settings")   Sets the file attributes of the file(s) according to the settings. Use uppercase to set the attribute, lowercase to clear it. (Version 2.0) **Example:**

    ; The following will make all the chapter files read only
    filespec = "D:\WP51\NDWREF*.CHP"
    FileAttrSet(filespec, "R")

FileClose(filehandle)   Closes a file that has been opened. Takes as an argument the filehandle returned from FileOpen. **Example:**

    handle = FileOpen("junk.txt","READ")

FileClose(handle)

FileCopy(sourcelist, destination, @TRUE ¦ @FALSE)
Copies a file or files. May display a warning message before over-writing an existing file if desired. Uses separate multiple source files with a space. Wildcards may also be used for the destination file name(s). **Example:**

**FileCopy("c:\junk.tmp c:\temp\junk.txt",
"c:\garbage\junk.*", @FALSE)**

FileDelete(filelist)   Deletes the specified files if they are not read only. Will return an error if the file is a hidden or system file, or if the file does not exist. Returns @TRUE if successful, @FALSE if not. Wildcards are acceptable, and you can separate filenames with spaces. **Example:**

FileDelete("*.bak *.bk? *.tmp")

FileExist((d:)(path)filename)   Tests to see if a file exists. Returns @TRUE if it does exist, @FALSE if not. Use this to make your batch files more bulletproof, since many Windows Batch Language commands will cause a fatal error if the file doesn't exist. **Example:**

delfile = FileExist("swap.sw2")
If delfile == @TRUE Then FileDelete("swap.sw2")

FileExtension(filename)   Takes as its argument a string whose value is a filename and, optionally, its path, including its extension, returning a string whose value is the extension. **Example:**

**filevar = AskLine("FileView", "What file did you want to
view?", "")**
filext = FileExtension(filevar)
If (filext == "exe") ¦¦ (filext == "com") Then Goto Sorry
Run("nviewer.exe", filevar)
Exit
:Sorry
**Message("Sorry", "Sorry, but there isn't really anything to
see with an executable file.")**

FileItemize(filelist) Takes a list of filenames, which may include names with wildcards, and returns a complete list of files that meet the criteria, separated by spaces. Especially useful with *ItemSelect*, which takes a list of items separated by spaces as its argument. **Example:**

```
;Choose from a list of files to edit when starting
;Word Perfect.
wpfiles = FileItemize("c:\wp51\ndw\*.chp")
editfile = ItemSelect("Which Chapter?", wpfiles, " ")
Run("wp.pif",editfile)
```

FileLocate(filename) Searches for a file in the current directory or anywhere along the DOS path. Returns the full filename, including complete path. **Example:**

```
editfile = FileLocate("ndw.ini")
Run("notepad.exe", editfile)
```

FileMove(sourcelist, destination, @TRUE ¦ @FALSE)
Copies a file or files and deletes the source file(s). May display a warning message before overwriting an existing file, if desired. To move multiple source files, separate them with a space. You may use wildcards. Use @TRUE if a warning is to be issued before overwriting an existing file and @FALSE if no warning is desired. Returns @TRUE if successful, @FALSE if not. **Example:**

```
FileMove("c:\win\*.ini", "d:\winfiles", @TRUE)
```

FileOpen(filename, "READ" ¦ "WRITE") Used to open a file for use by the FileRead or FileWrite functions. The file must be an ASCII file. The function returns a special integer value (filehandle) which can then be used by the FileRead, FileWrite, or FileClose functions. When finished reading from or writing to the file, use FileClose to close it. **Example:**

```
; Opens autoexec.bat for reading, with a filehandle
; assigned to the variable "filevar".
filevar = FileOpen("c:\autoexec.bat", "READ")
```

FilePath(filename) Takes a full filename, including path, and strips out the filename, leaving only the path portion. **Example:**

```
ini = FileLocate("win.ini")
```

```
inipath = FilePath(ini)
```

FileRead(filehandle)   Returns a line of text as a single string each time it is invoked. When the end of the file is reached, it returns "*EOF*". The file to read from is identified by the filehandle returned by the FileOpen function. **Example:**

```
filevar = FileOpen ("junk.txt", "READ")
:begin
LineOfText = FileRead(filevar) Display (3, "Junk.Txt",
LineOfText)
If LineOfText != "*EOF*" Then Goto begin
FileClose (filevar)
```

FileRename(sourcelist, destination)   Changes the name of a file or files. You can use wildcards in the source list and the * wildcard for the destination. Unlike FileMove, you cannot rename across drives. **Example:**

```
FileRename ("c:\autoexec.bat", "autoexec.sav")
```

FileRoot(filename)   Takes a filename, including its extension, and strips out the period and the extension, returning only the root. Includes the full pathname if it was part of the filename. **Example:**

```
inifile = FileLocate("win.ini")
iniroot = FileRoot(inifile)
```

FileSize(filelist)   Takes a list of files, separated by spaces, as its argument and returns the total number of bytes taken by the files. Does not accept wildcards, but you can use FileItemize to generate the list. **Example:**

```
baksize = FileSize(FileItemize ("*.bak"))
Display(4,"Space Wasted by BAK files", baksize)
```

FileTimeGet("filename")   Returns a string whose value is equal to a file's time and date in Windows' short format (set with the International section of the Control Panel). (Version 2.0) **Example:**

```
when = FileTimeGet("c:\config.sys")
```

```
Message("Status", "The configuration file was last
changed on %when%")
```

FileTimeTouch(filename)   Changes a file's time and date to the current time and date. (Version 2.0) **Example:**

```
winfile = StrCat(DirWindows(0), "WIN.INI")
FileTimeTouch(winfile)
when = FileTimeGet(winfile)
Message("Update", "The timestamp on %winfile% is
%when%")
```

FileWrite(filehandle,outputtext)   Writes a line of text to an ASCII file each time it is invoked. The file to write to is identified by the filehandle returned from the FileOpen function. **Example:**

```
stuff = AskLine("Stuff to Write", "What would you like to
write in STUFF.TXT? ", "")
filevar = FileOpen("stuff.txt", "WRITE")
FileWrite (filevar,stuff)
FileClose(filevar)
```

Goto *label*   Causes the batch file to branch, unconditionally, to the line identified by the label. Labels begin with a colon in the first position of the line and may not include any embedded spaces. **Example:**

```
If WinExist("WordPerfect") == @FALSE Then Goto openwp
WinActivate("WordPerfect")
Goto end
:openwp
Run("wp.pif", "")
:end
```

IconArrange()   Arranges the icons on the desktop along the bottom of the screen. (Version 2.0) **Example:**

```
IconArrange()
```

If *condition* **Then** *statement*   Used to test for the value of a condition. If the condition is true, then the statement will be executed. If the condition is false, then the statement is skipped and the next line of the batch file is executed. **Example:**

> **If WinExist("Desktop Editor") == @TRUE Then Goto activate**
> **inifile = FileItemize("c:\win*.ini")**
> **editfile = ItemSelect("Which .INI File?", inifile, " ")**
> **Run("deskedit.exe",editfile)**
> **Goto end**
> **:activate**
> **WinActivate("Desktop Editor")**
> **:end**

IgnoreInput(@TRUE ¦ @FALSE)   Causes Windows to ignore all mouse movements and keystrokes when set to @TRUE. Returns to normal by setting to @FALSE. Use with extreme caution, because a mistake will crash the computer! **Example:**

> **IgnoreInput(@TRUE)**
> **Display(15,"PATIENCE!", "This will take 15 seconds, and nothing you can do will make it go faster!")**
> **IgnoreInput(@FALSE)**

● **NOTE**   This does not work in Version 1.0, and in Version 2.0, only input to the batch file is ignored. Other processes can still receive input.

IniDelete("section", "keyword")   Deletes the line beginning with "keyword" from the WIN.INI file section beginning with "section". (Version 2.0) **Example:**

> **IniDelete("windows", "load")**

IniDeletePvt("section", "keyword", "filename")   Works like IniDelete, except can be used on any .INI file. (Version 2.0) **Example:**

> **IniDeletePvt("NortonDesktop", "ToolsTile", "winfile.ini")**

IniItemize("Section")   Returns a string whose value is equal to a tab delimited list of keywords in the section of the WIN.INI file. If "Section" is "" then returns a tab delimited list of the section names in WIN.INI. (Version 2.0) **Example:**

```
tab = Num2Char(09)
seclist = IniItemize("")
section = ItemSelect("Which Section?", seclist, tab)
keylist = IniItemize(section)
delkey = ItemSelect("Which Keyword?", keylist, tab)
confirm = AskYesNo("Confirm", "Are you sure you want
to delete %delkey% in the %section% section")
If confirm Then IniDelete(section,delkey)
```

IniItemizePvt("Section", "filename")   Works   like   Ini-
Itemize, except can be used with any .INI file. (Version 2.0) **Example:**

```
seclist = IniItemizePvt("", "ndw.ini")
section = ItemSelect("NDW.INI Sections", seclist,
Num2Char(09))
```

IniRead(section, keyname, default)   Allows you to read
data from the WIN.INI file. If the specified data is not found, returns
the default string. **Example:**

```
beepstat = IniRead("windows", "Beep", "Yes")
If beepstat == "No" Then Goto beepoff
Beep
Beep
Beep
Goto end
:beepoff
Display(3,"BEEP!", "You have Beeps turned OFF!")
:end
```

IniReadPvt(section, keyname, default, filename)
Allows you to read data from a private .INI file. Works like IniRead.
Example:

```
save = IniReadPvt("CONFIGURATION", "SAVE", "TRUE",
"ndw.ini")
```

IniWrite(section, keyname, data)   Allows you to write data
to your WIN.INI file. If the section is not found, it will create it. If the

keyname is already present, it will overwrite it. **Example:**

> IniWrite("windows", "Beep", "yes")

IniWritePvt(section, keyname, data, filename)   Allows you to write data to a private .INI file. Works like IniWrite. **Example:**

> IniWritePvt("boot", "shell", "c:\ndw\ndw.exe",
> "c:\win\system.ini")

IsDefined(var)   Tests to see if a variable is currently defined. If it is, it returns @TRUE. If it has never been defined, or has been dropped, it returns @FALSE. **Example:**

> defined = IsDefined(anyvar)
> If defined == @TRUE Then Goto OK
> anyvar = AskLine("Definition", "What is the value of ANYVAR?", "something")
> :OK

IsKeyDown(keycode)   Used to test the current state of the Shift or Ctrl key. If the specified key is held down, @YES is returned. If not, @NO is returned. Accepts the right mouse button for Shift and the left button for Ctrl. **Example:**

> ;The following requires both the Shift and the Ctrl keys
> ;to be pressed.
> IsKeyDown(@CTRL & @SHIFT)
> ;This one only requires that the Ctrl key be pressed
> IsKeyDown(@CTRL)
> ;And this one accepts either key
> IsKeyDown(@CTRL | @SHIFT)

IsNumber(stringvar)   Checks a string and tests whether it is valid as an integer. Used for checking user input before acting on it. Returns @YES if it is an integer, @NO if it is not. **Example:**

> :getnum
> int = AskLine("How Many", "How many times should I do this?", "1")
> If IsNumber(int) == @NO Then Goto getnum

192 The Norton Windows Batch Language

ItemCount(list, delimiter)   Counts the number of items in a list. Takes the list and a delimiter as its arguments. **Example:**

    dirlist = DirItemize("c:*")
    dircount = ItemCount(dirlist, " ")
    Display(3, "INFO", "There are %dircount% directories.")

ItemExtract(position, list, delimiter)   Evaluates a list and extracts an item from it, based on its position in the list. **Example:**

    filelist = FileItemize("*.*")
    first = ItemExtract(1, filelist, " ")

ItemSelect(title, list, delimiter)   Draws a list box and allows user to select an item from the list. Returns a string whose value is the item selected from the list. **Example:**

    inifile = FileItemize("c:\win*.ini")
    editfile = ItemSelect("Which .INI File?", inifile, " ")
    Run("deskedit.exe",editfile)

LastError()   Returns the error code for the most recent error. Will not work with fatal errors, because they will cancel execution of the batch file. **Example:**

    ErrorMode(@OFF)
    close = WinClose("Notepad")
    If close == @True Then Goto end
    if LastError() == 1039 Then Display(2,"ERROR", "Window wasn't open!")
    :end

LogDisk(drive)   Changes disk drives. Returns @TRUE if successful, @FALSE if not. **Example:**

    LogDisk("e:")

Max(integer(, integer)…)   Evaluates a list of integers, separated by commas, and returns the largest integer in the list. **Example:**

    maxnum = Max(17, –23, 45, 6)

Display(3, "Largest number is:", maxnum)

Message(title, text)   Displays a message until the user clicks on **OK**. Unlike Display, it stops processing of the batch file indefinitely. **Example:**

Message("The current path is:", Environment ("PATH"))

Min(integer(, integer)...)   Evaluates a list of integers, separated by commas, and returns the smallest. **Example:**

minnum = Min(17, −23, 45, 6)
Display(3, "Smallest number is:", minnum)

MouseInfo(flag)   Returns various information about the mouse, depending on the value of "flag". If flag = 0, returns the name of the window under the mouse; if flag = 1, returns the top-level parent of the window under the mouse; if flag = 2, returns the mouse coordinates (assumes a virtual 1000×1000 screen); if flag = 3, returns the absolute coordinates of the mouse; and if flag = 4, returns the status of the mouse buttons, where 0 = no buttons down, 1 = right button down, 2 = middle button down, 3 = right and middle buttons down, 4 = left button down, 5 = left and right buttons down, 6 = left and middle buttons down, and 7 = all buttons down. (Version 2.0) **Example:**

windname = MouseInfo(1)
Message("WindowName", "The window under the mouse is %windname%")

NetAddCon(netpath, password, localname)   Connects network resource to a drive letter or printer port. Returns @TRUE if successful, @FALSE if not. (Version 2.0) **Example:**

result = NetAddCon("\\MAINSERVER\C-DRIVE", "", "G:")

NetAttach("server")   Attaches workstation to server. Novell NetWare only. (Version 2.0) **Example:**

NetAttach("MAINSERVER")

NetBrowse(flag)   Displays dialog for user to select a network resource (if flag = 0) or a print queue (if flag = 1). Returns a string whose value is equal to the network resource name selected. (Ver-

194 The Norton Windows Batch Language

sion 2.0) **Example:**

   selectQ = NetBrowse(1)

NetCancelCon(Name,Force)   Cancels the connection with "Name" where "Name" is either the local name or the network resource name. If Force = 0, will fail if there are open files, if Force = 1, will break the connection regardless of file status. (Version 2.0) **Example:**

   NetCancelCon("G:", 0)

NetDetach(server)   With Novell Netware, detaches the workstation from the server. (Version 2.0) **Example:**

   NetDetach("MAINSERVER")

NetDialog()   Displays the network's access dialog box. (Version 2.0) **Example:**

   NetDialog()

NetGetCon(LocalName)   Returns the network resource name for the resource connected to LocalName. (Version 2.0) **Example:**

   servername = NetGetCon("W:")
   Message("Resource Name", "The network resource name for W: is %servername%.")

NetGetUser()   Returns a string whose value is equal to the names of the users currently logged in. (Version 2.0) **Example:**

   who = NetGetUser()
   Message("Users", "The users logged in currently are %who%.")

NetLogin(servername,username,password)   Logs a user onto a server, using the password contained in the variable "password". (Version 2.0) **Example:**

   server = "MAINSERVER"
   mypassword = AskPassword("Login", "Please enter your password for %server%.")
   NetLogin(server, "CHARLIE", mypassword)

NetLogout(servername) Logs the current user off of servername. (Version 2.0) **Example:**

> server = "MAINSERVER"
> NetLogout(server)

NetMapRoot("driveletter", "server\volume:path")
Redirects a drive letter to substitute for the network path. Novell Netware only. (Version 2.0) **Example:**

> NetMapRoot("W:", "MAINSERVER\VOL:PUBLIC")

NetMemberGet(server, group) Returns the value @TRUE if the current user is a member of group on server. Returns @FALSE if not. (Version 2.0) **Example:**

> IsMember = NetMemberGet("MAINSERVER", "USERS")
> If IsMember Then NetLogin("MAINSERVER", username, userpswd)

NetMemberSet(server,group) Assigns the current user to the group on server. (Version 2.0) **Example:**

> NetMemberSet("MAINSERVER", "USERS")

NetMsgAll("server", "message") Sends a message to all the users on server. (Version 2.0) **Example:**

> NetMsgAll("MAINSERVER", "System will be shutdown in 10 Minutes for Maintenance")

NetMsgSend("server", "user", "message") Sends a message to an individual user on server. Otherwise works like NetMsgAll. (Version 2.0) **Example:**

> NetMsgSend("MAINSERVER", "ALFIE", "Can we meet at 2PM?")

Num2Char(integer) Used to change an integer to its ASCII equivalent. Accepts any integer from 0 to 255. Extremely useful for converting control codes to a string for inclusion in string variables. **Example:**

> crlf = StrCat(Num2Char(13), Num2Char(10))

```
Message("Two Line Box", "This is a line of text.
%crlf%This is another line of text.")
```

ParseData(string)   Chops a string up into substrings. Assumes spaces are the delimiter, and stores each "word" in param1, param2...param*n*, with the total count (*n*) stored inparam0. **Example:**

```
crlf = StrCat(Num2Char(13), Num2Char(10))
user = AskLine("NAME?", "What is your name, please?",
"Jane Doe")
ParseData(user)
If param0 == 1 Then Goto single
If param0 == 2 Then Goto double
name = param3
Goto end
:single
name = param1
Goto end
:double
name = param2
:end
Message("UserName", " Since we are rather formal
here, %crlf% your name on this system will be:
%name%")
```

Pause(title, text)   Draws a message box and displays a text message in it until the user selects either **OK** or **Cancel**. This is similar to the Message instruction except for the Cancel option and the inclusion of an exclamation-point icon. **Example:**

```
Pause("Ready?", "Insert disk to copy into Drive A:")
```

Random(max)   Takes a maximum number as its parameter and returns a pseudorandom positive number less than that maximum. **Example:**

```
ran = Random(126)
Display(3,"Random number less than 126", ran)
```

Return   Returns control to the calling batch file. If there is no calling batch file, then Exit is performed.

Run(programname, parameters)   Starts a program in its normal window. If the program is not an executable file (.COM, .EXE, .BAT, or .PIF) then it must have an association to an executable file. If the file has an extension of .EXE, then the extension may be omitted. **Example:**

```
Run("notepad", "win.ini")
Run("c:\ndw\editfile.wbt", "*.ini")
```

RunHide(programname, parameters)   Same as Run except that it attempts to run the program in a hidden window. **Example:**

```
RunHide("sleeper", "")
```

RunIcon(programname, parameters)   Same as Run except that it iconizes the program. **Example:**

```
;Run AfterDark as an icon
RunIcon("ad","")
```

RunZoom(programname, parameters)   Same as Run except that it zooms the program to full screen. **Example:**

```
RunZoom("c:\borland\vision.exe","")
```

SendKey(charstring)   Used to pass keystrokes to the active program. Can be used to send any alphanumeric character, as well as the punctuation marks and special characters shown in Table 5.1. **Example:**

```
;Open Borland's Object Vision, and go to the
;File Open menu, looking for *.OVD files
RunIcon("c:\borland\vision.exe", "")
SendKey("!FO*.ovd")
```

Table V.1: Special Characters for SendKey

Key	SendKey Equivalent
~	{~}
!	{!}
^	{^}
+	{+}
Backspace	{BACKSPACE} or {BS}
Break	{BREAK}
Clear	{CLEAR}
Delete	{DELETE} or {DEL}
↓	{DOWN}
End	{END}
Enter	{ENTER} or ~
Escape	{ESCAPE} or {ESC}
F1–F16	{F1} through {F16}
Help	{HELP}
Home	{HOME}
Insert	{INSERT}
←	{LEFT}
Page Down	{PGDN}
Page Up	{PGUP}
→	{RIGHT}
Space	{SPACE} or {SP}
Tab	{TAB}
↑	{UP}

To enter an **Alt**, **Shift**, *or* **Ctrl** *key combination, use the following symbols before the character you want. Alt = ! (exclamation point); Shift = + (plus sign); Control = ^ (caret).*

SKDebug(mode)   Controls the debug mode of SendKey. If SKDebug is set to @ON, the keystrokes are sent to both the application and a file. If set to @PARSEONLY, it sends the keystrokes to the file but not to the application. If set to the default, @OFF, then it sends the keystrokes only to the application. The default filename for SKDebug to use is C:\@@SKDBUG.TXT, but this can be controlled by making an entry in WIN.INI, such as:

(Batch Runner)
SKDFile=c:\win\debug.key

Example:

Run("wp.pif", "")
If WinConfig() & 32 Then Goto enhanced
Goto end
:enhanced
SKDebug (@ON)
;You can only pass keystrokes in 386 Enhanced
;mode to a DOS Application.
SendKey ("{F5}")
SKDebug (@OFF)
:end

SnapShot(flag)   Copies the image in the window designated by flag to the Windows Clipboard. If flag = 0, the entire screen is copied; if flag = 1, the client area of the parent of the active window is copied; if flag = 2, the parent of the active window is copied; if flag = 3, the client area of the active window is copied; and if flag = 4, the entire active window is copied to the Clipboard. (Version 2.0) **Example:**

SnapShot(4)

Sounds(@ON!@OFF)   Turns Multimedia sounds on or off. Returns the previous state. (Windows 3.1 only) (Version 2.0) **Example:**

laststate = Sounds(@ON)

StrCat(string1, string2(, string3)...)   Joins two or more strings together into a single string. **Example:**

```
crlf = StrCat(Num2Char(13), Num2Char(10))
```

StrCmp(string1, string2)   Evaluates and compares two strings. Requires an exact match, including case. Returns −1 if string1 is less than string2, 0 if they are the same, and 1 if string1 is greater than string2, using ANSI equivalency for the test. Note that the same thing can be accomplished using the relational operators, >, ≥, ==, !=, <, ≤. **Example:**

```
filename = AskLine("Edit Filename", "What File would
you like to Edit?", "WIN.INI")
If StrCmp(StrLower(filename), "win.ini") != 0 Then Goto
notini
Run("notepad",filename)
Goto end :notini
editor = AskLine("Editor?", "What editor would you like
to use?", "")
Run(editor, filename)
:end
```

StrFill(fillstr, length)   Builds a filler string of specified length using substring as the filler. **Example:**

```
Display(3,"Money!", StrFill("$", 60))
```

StrFix(initstring, padstring, length)   Creates a string of the specified length either by padding the initial string with the padding string or by chopping off the initial string at the specified length, counting from the left. **Example:**

```
name = StrFix("Frank", "*", 20)
Display(5,"",name)
```

StrICmp(string1, string2)   Like StrCmp, but it is not case-sensitive. Returns −1 if string1 is less than string2, 0 if they are the same, and 1 if string1 is greater than string2, using ANSI equivalency for the test. **Example:**

```
If StrICmp("Alfie", "ALFIE") == 0 Then Goto SAME
```

```
Message("Compare", "Alfie is not the same as ALFIE.")
Exit
:SAME
Message("Compare", "Alfie is the same as ALFIE.")
```

StrIndex(string, substring, start, direction)   Searches for a substring of a string and returns the position of the substring. Returns 0 if the string is not found. Can search in either direction, starting from any point in the string. To start at the beginning, direction will be @FWDSCAN and start position will be 0. To start at the end of the string, direction will be @BACKSCAN and start position will be 0. **Example:**

```
strvar = AskLine("String Index", "Type a sentence:", "")
start = 1
end = StrIndex(strvar, " ", start, @FWDSCAN)
word = StrSub(strvar, start, end –1)
Message("String Index", "The first word is: %word%.")
```

StrLen(string)   Evaluates a string and returns an integer whose value is the length of the string. **Example:**

```
strvar = AskLine("String Length", "Type in a sentence or
two.", "")
length = StrLen(strvar)
Message("String Length", "The string you typed in is
%length% characters long.")
```

StrLower(string)   Changes a string to all lowercase. **Example:**

```
StrLower("This is a SilLY sTRinG Which NEEds tO be fIXeD.")
```

StrReplace(string, old, new)   Does a search and replace. Replaces all occurrences of one string with another. **Example:**

```
filelist = FileItemize("*.wbt")
crlf = StrCat(Num2Char(13), Num2Char(10))
newlist = StrReplace (filelist, " ", crlf)
filevar = FileOpen("wbatlist.txt", "WRITE")
FileWrite(filevar, newlist)
```

FileClose(filevar)

TextBox("Windows Batch Files", "wbatlist.txt")

StrScan(string, delimiters, start, direction) Evaluates a string, looking for a particular delimiter or set of delimiters. Returns the position of the first occurrence found; if no occurrences are found, returns 0. **Example:**

strvar = AskLine("String Scan", "Enter a series of numbers, separated by commas or semicolons.", "")

firstnum = StrScan(strvar, ",;", 1, @FWDSCAN)

Display(3, "String Scan", "The first number is %firstnum%.")

StrSub(string, start, length) Evaluates a string, and extracts a substring from it. **Example:**

strvar = AskLine("SubString", "Enter a sentence, please.", "")

firstword = StrSub(strvar, 1, StrScan(strvar, " ", 1, @FWDSCAN))

Display(3, "First Word", "The first word is: %firstword%")

StrTrim(string) Strips all leading and trailing spaces from a string. Use it to clean up user input where it could be a problem, such as with a filename. **Example:**

filename = StrTrim(StrLower(AskLine("File?", "Enter the file to edit?", "")))

StrUpper(string) Evaluates a string and changes it all to upper-case. **Example:**

response = StrUpper(AskLine("Proceed?", "Type yes to proceed, all else cancels", "NO"))

If response != "YES" Then Exit

TextBox(title, filename) Draws a list box and displays a file in it. Also allows the user to select a line, which it then returns to the batch file. TextBox will search the DOS path if the file specified is not found in the current drive and directory. **Example:**

> **var = TextBox ("Choose a Line", "c:\autoexec.bat")**
> **Display(3,"Chosen Line", var)**

Version() Finds the current version of BATCHRUN.EXE. **Example:**

> **batver = Version()**
>
> **Display(3,"Current Version", "The current version of BatchRunner is: %batver%")**

WaitForKey("char","char","char","char","char") Waits for one of 5 keystrokes. Returns the number of the parameter. Use ! for right alt, ^ for control and + for shifted. Must have all parameters. Use "" for empty parameters. Uses same syntax as SendKey. Useful for controlling branching operations based on user input. (Version 2.0) **Example:**

> **reply = WaitForKey("A", "B", "C", "", "")**
>
> **IF reply = 1 THEN GoTo choiceA**
>
> **IF reply = 2 THEN GoTo choiceB**
>
> **AskYesNo("Response", "You chose option C. Is this correct?")**
>
> **GoTo end**
>
> **:choiceA**
>
> **AskYesNo("Response", "You chose option A. Is this correct?")**
>
> **GoTo end**
>
> **:choiceB**
>
> **AskYesNo("Response", "You chose option B. Is this correct?")**
>
> **:end**

WallPaper(bmpname, tile) Changes the current wallpaper used on the desktop and determines if it is to be tiled or not. **Example:**

> **filelist = FileItemize("c:\win*.bmp")**

```
bmpvar = ItemSelect("Select your new background",
filelist, " ")
WallPaper(bmpvar, @FALSE)
```

WinActivate(partialwindowname)   Activates the specified window or icon, making it the current window. The most recently used window or icon that matches the partial window name is activated. If the specified window is an icon, it restores it; if it is already a window, it makes it the current window, but does not change the size. Note that this function requires an exact match of the partial window name and is case sensitive. Returns @TRUE if successful, @FALSE if not. **Example:**

```
If WinExist("WordPerfect") Then Goto activate
Run("wp.pif", "")
Goto end
:activate
WinActivate("WordPerfect")
:end
```

WinArrange(style)   Arranges all open windows on the desktop (up to 12). Does not rearrange iconized windows. Accepts one of five different styles: @STACK, @TILE, @ARRANGE (same as @TILE), @ROWS, and @COLUMNS. **Example:**

```
WinArrange(@TILE)
```

WinClose(partialwindowname)   Closes a window or icon. Like WinActivate, it takes a partial window name, which must be an exact match and which is case sensitive. Returns @TRUE if successful, @FALSE if not. **Example:**

```
WinClose("Notepad")
```

WinConfig()   Returns the sum of Windows' mode flags. These flags are the following:

1	Protected mode
2	80286 CPU
4	80386 CPU

8	80486 CPU
16	Standard mode
32	Enhanced mode
64	8086 CPU
128	80186 CPU
256	Large PageFrame
512	Small PageFrame
1024	Math Coprocessor installed

Example:

```
currentcfg = WinConfig()
If currentcfg & 8 Then Display(3,"CPU", "This machine
has an 80486 Processor.")
```

WinExeName(partialwindowname)   Returns the .EXE filename (including drive and path) of the owner of the window. (Version 2.0) **Example:**

```
name = WinExeName("After")
Message("NAME", "After Dark's executible file is
%name%")
```

WinExist(partialwindowname)   Checks for the presence of a particular window or icon. Returns @TRUE if found, @FALSE if not. **Example:**

```
If WinExist("QPro") == @FALSE Then Run("QP.PIF", "")
```

WinGetActive()   Finds the title of the active window. **Example:**

```
curwin = WinGetActive()
```

WinHide(partialwindowname)   Used to hide a window or icon. When hidden, the programs continue to run. A partial window name of "" causes the current window to be hidden. Returns @TRUE if successful, @FALSE if not. **Example:**

```
WinHide("Sleeper")
```

WinIconize(partialwindowname) Minimizes a window. Like WinHide, a partial window name of "" causes the active window to be iconized. Returns @TRUE if successful, @FALSE if not. **Example:**

```
Run("clock.exe", "")
WinIconize("Clo")
```

WinItemize( ) Creates a list of the titles of all open windows, separated by tabs. Behaves similarly to FileItemize and DirItemize except for the use of tabs as delimiters, because window titles can have embedded spaces. **Example:**

```
winopen = WinItemize()
winchoose = ItemSelect ("Windows", winopen,
Num2Char(9))
WinActive(winchoose)
```

WinName( ) Returns the window title of the active window. (Version 2.0) **Example:**

```
current = WinName()
```

WinPlace(x-ulc, y-ulc, x-brc, y-brc, partialwindowname) Places the window in a specified location and sets the size as well. Size is controlled by four parameters: x-ulc, the distance from the upper-left corner of the window to the left of the screen (0–1000); y-ulc, the distance from the upper-left corner of the window to the top of the screen (0–1000); x-brc, the distance from the bottom-right corner of the window to the left of the screen (10–1000 or @NORESIZE); and y-brc, the distance from the bottom-right corner of the window to the top of the screen (10–1000, @NORESIZE, or @ABOVEICONS). **Example:**

```
WinPlace(700,0,200,200,"Clock")
```

WinPlaceGet(win-type, partialwindowname) Returns the normal, iconized, or zoomed coordinates of the window, depending on the win-type (@NORMAL, @ICON, or @ZOOMED). (Windows 3.1) (Version 2.0) **Example:**

```
location = WinPlaceGet(@NORMAL, "DeskEdit")
```

WinPlaceSet(win-type, partialwindowname, new-coords)
Assigns the coordinates of the window, based on the window type. Uses the same coordinate syntax as WinPlace. (Windows 3.1) (Version 2.0) **Example:**

> location = "700, 0, 200, 200"
> WinPlace(@ICON, "Clock", location)

WinPosition(partialwindowname)
Finds the coordinates of the specified window. **Example:**

> WinPosition("Clock")

WinResources(flag)
Returns the current Windows resources. Returns memory available (in bytes) if flag = 0; theoretical maximum memory if flag = 1; percentage of free system resources if flag = 2; GDI if flag =3; and user resources if flag = 4. (Version 2.0) **Example:**

> rsrc = WinResources(2)
> Message("WinStat", "There are still %rsrc% %% Windows resources available.")

WinShow(partialwindowname)
Returns the specified window to normal size and position. **Example:**

> WinShow("PageMaker")

WinState("partial window name")
Returns the current state of the window, −1 if hidden, 0 if it doesn't exist, 1 if iconized, 2 if normal and 3 if zoomed. (Version 2.0) **Example:**

> status = WinState("ObjectVision")
> IF status == 0 THEN Run("D:\OV2\OV.EXE","")
> WinActivate("ObjectVision")

WinTitle(partialwindowname, newname)
Renames window or icon by changing its window title. Returns @TRUE if successful, @FALSE if not. **Caution:** Some programs will not behave well if their window title is changed. **Example:**

> WinTitle("QPro", "Quattro Pro 4.0")

WinVersion(@MAJOR!@MINOR) Finds what version of Windows is running. @MAJOR returns the integer portion of the version and @MINOR returns the decimal portion. **Example:**

> ver = WinVersion(@MINOR)
> Message("Version", StrCat("Windows Version 3.", ver))

WinWaitClose(partialwindowname) Halts the running of the batch file while it waits for the specified window or icon to close. Closes all windows or icons that match the partial window name. Returns @TRUE if successful, @FALSE if not.

WinZoom(partialwindowname) Zooms a window to full screen. Returns @TRUE if successful, @FALSE if not. **Example:**

> WinZoom("Note")

Yield Provides clock cycles for other windows to do processing. This is one way to make your batch files better behaved, allowing other Windows processes to run concurrently.

Part Six

The Fix-It Disk Programs

You run the Fix-It Disk programs from the DOS prompt. If you are trying to repair or restore your hard disk or to recover deleted files, the programs must be run from a floppy drive because

- Speed Disk and the active portions of Norton Disk Doctor cannot be run safely in a multitasking environment such as Windows.

- If you have deleted unprotected files, starting Windows to run UnErase can cause the files to be overwritten and, therefore, make them unrecoverable.

- If you have accidentally formatted your hard disk, you will not be able to access UnFormat if it is (or was) on your hard disk—it can be run only from a floppy.

EMERGENCY RESTORE

The Emergency Restore program (Version 2.0 only) will let you restore a full backup without having to re-install any programs. See *Backup* in *Part Four* for instructions.

NORTON DISK DOCTOR

Disk Doctor should be used in the following cases:

- When you have trouble accessing a disk, or a disk behaves erratically.

- When files or directories seem to be missing but were not deleted.

- When you want to practice preventive maintenance to look for budding problems.

To Diagnose a Disk

1. Insert the Fix-It Disk into the floppy drive. Change to that drive. At the DOS prompt, key in

   ndd

2. In the Norton Disk Doctor window, click on **Diagnose Disk.**

3. Click on the drive(s) that you want to test. Use the spacebar or mouse to select and deselect drives. A check-mark will appear beside the selected drives.

4. Click on **Diagnose**. The tests being performed will be listed on the screen with checkmarks appearing next to the tests as they are completed. The following parts of the hard disk are tested:

   Partition Table: Information on how the hard disk is divided.

   Boot Record: The portion of the disk that identifies the disk and contains the programs from which DOS boots.

   File Allocation Table (FAT): The part of the disk where file locations are tracked.

   Directory Structure: Information about directory organization.

   File Structure: Information about the organization of the files.

   Lost Clusters: Clusters that are recorded in the FAT but do not belong to a file or directory.

5. If errors are detected and you want Disk Doctor to correct them, you will be prompted to create an UnDo file just in case the changes that take place are not quite what you expect.

6. When the Surface Test window opens, select the tests you wish to perform. To change the Surface Test default options, see *To Set Disk Doctor Options*, below.

7. When the tests are finished, select **Report** from the Summary window to generate a report of the test results or select **Done** to exit. If you select **Report** you can view, print, or save the report to a file name of your choosing.

To UnDo Changes

1. Start Disk Doctor. Select **UnDo Changes** from the Norton Disk Doctor window.

2. Read the explanation and if you want to continue, select **Yes.**

3. Select the drive where the undo information was previously stored and click **OK.** Follow the instructions to undo the Disk Doctor operations.

To Set Disk Doctor Options

1. Start Disk Doctor. Select **Options** in the Norton Disk Doctor window.

2. In the Disk Doctor Options window, select the options you want to configure.

3. When finished, select **Save Settings** to make your choices permanent.

● OPTIONS: SURFACE TESTS

In the Test area, select **Disk Test** to test the entire disk. Select **File Test** to test only the areas being used by existing files. Note that Disk Test is slower, but more thorough than File Test.

In the Test Type area, the **Daily** option is a quick scan. The **Weekly** option is slower but more thorough. **Auto Weekly** is the default setting and is a daily test except on Fridays, when the Weekly test is performed.

In the Passes area, select **Repetitions** and key in the number of passes to specify the number of times Disk Doctor should search the disk. For an extended test, select **Continuous,** and the search will proceed until you press **Esc** to end it.

In the Repair Setting area, select **Don't Repair** if you want a diagnosis but do not want any fixes. Select **Prompt before Repairing** and Disk Doctor will report the error and ask if

you want the error fixed. If you want Disk Doctor to make
repairs without prompting, choose **Repair Automatically**.

● OPTIONS: CUSTOM MESSAGE

When Disk Doctor finds an error, it displays an error and correction
message. To substitute your own message, select **Custom Message.**
Note that after a custom message is displayed, you cannot proceed;
instead, you will be returned to the Main menu after selecting **OK.**
Custom messages are useful for system administrators who want to
be notified when errors are diagnosed.

● OPTIONS: TESTS TO SKIP

Toggle **Skip Partition Tests** on if your system uses nonstandard partition software.

Select **Skip CMOS Tests** if you are using a nonstandard CMOS
format.

Toggle **Skip Surface Tests** on if you always want to skip surface testing.

Check **Only 1 Hard Disk** if your computer reports more than
one hard disk and you have only one.

● **NOTE**   You can run the Disk Doctor from a network, but you
will not be able to test network drives. Also, Norton Disk Doctor will
not work on disks having 1024 or more cylinders.

To Use Disk Doctor from the Command Line

● SYNTAX
NDD (drive:)… (/C) (/Q) (/R(A):pathname) (/X:drives)
NDD (drive:)… (/REBUILD)
NDD (drive)… (/UNDELETE)

drive specifies the disk drive to be diagnosed or repaired.
More than one drive can be listed.

/C specifies a complete test, including the partition table, boot
record, root directory, lost clusters, and the default surface tests.

/Q specifies all tests except the surface tests.

/R[A]:pathname writes (or appends) a report of the tests performed to the named file.

/X:drives excludes named drives from testing.

/REBUILD rebuilds a destroyed disk.

/UNDELETE undeletes a previously skipped DOS partition.

SPEED DISK

Speed Disk is a disk-optimization program that rearranges files and directories to minimize the movement of the hard disk read/write head. Back up your files as an added safety measure before running Speed Disk on your computer for the first time.

To Run Speed Disk

1. Insert the Fix-It Disk into the appropriate floppy drive. Change to that drive. At the DOS prompt, key in

   speedisk

2. The program will ask you to select a drive to optimize. Select a drive and click on **OK**.

3. After searching the drive, Speed Disk will ask if you want to optimize the drive or to configure Speed Disk.

4. If you select **Optimize**, the program will continue and inform you of its findings. If you want to change the Speed Disk settings, select **Configure**.

• OPTIONS: CONFIGURE MENU

Directory Order lets you select the order of directories on the disk.

File Sort allows you to select the sort criteria for files within directories. The default is unsorted.

Files To Place First opens a dialog box in which you can specify files to be placed at the front of the disk.

Unmovable Files specifies files, such as some copy-protected files, that should not be moved by Speed Disk.

Other Options

> **Read After Write** reads data back at once after it is written to verify accuracy. The default is on. Speed Disk will work faster if it is toggled off.

> **Clear unused space** writes zeroes in all unused clusters after optimization as a security measure.

> **Beep when done** sounds a beep when optimization is complete.

Save Options to Disk saves the current set of Speed Disk options to SD.INI, a hidden file in the root directory of the currently selected disk. These options will be in effect when you select a different disk and each time that you start up Speed Disk. The options saved are the optimization method; the physical directory and file placement; the file sort criterion; selection of immovable files; the verification method; and the clear unused space option.

● OPTIONS: INFORMATION MENU

Disk Statistics provides a report on the chosen drive, including the size of the drive, space used, clusters allocated, and so forth.

Map Legend provides a detailed disk map legend.

Show Static Files reports on files that Speed Disk has determined as unmovable during disk optimization.

Walk Map shows which files occupy which clusters on the disk map. Use the mouse or cursor control keys to "walk" around the map.

Fragmentation Report provides a report on which files are fragmented and to what degree.

• OPTIONS: OPTIMIZE MENU

Begin Optimization starts the optimization process.

Drive changes the drive choice.

Optimization Method allows you to select from the following five methods to optimize your disk:

- **Full Optimization** defragments all files without rearranging the directory or file sort. This method will fill all empty spaces between files.

- **Full with DIRs first** defragments files and moves directories to the front.

- **Full with File reorder** performs a full optimization of the disk, reordering files by directory. This is the most thorough and also the slowest method of optimization.

- **Unfragment Files Only** will unfragment as many files as possible. Not all holes will be filled and some large files may not be unfragmented.

- **Unfragment Free Space** will fill in free space but will not unfragment files.

To Use Speed Disk from the Command Line

• SYNTAX

SPEEDISK (drive:) (/F¦/FD¦/FF) (/Sorder) (/V) (/B)

SPEEDISK (drive:) (/Q¦/U) (/V) (/B)

/F	Full optimization
/FD	Full optimization, directories in front
/FF	Full optimization, files reordered
/Q	Unfragment free space (fastest option)
/U	Unfragment files only
/S	Sort files in the order specified

Order	One of the following:	
N		Name
E		Extension
D		Date and time
S		Size
Minus sign (–)		Sort in reverse order

/B	Reboot after optimization is complete
/V	After writing, verify by reading back immediately

UNERASE

UnErase can recover files automatically if they have remained intact. Files also can be recovered manually if they have become fragmented or have been partially overwritten.

To Automatically Recover Erased Files

1. Insert the Fix-It Disk in the floppy drive. Change to that drive. From the DOS prompt, key in

unerase

2. In the UnErase window, pull down the File menu to select the drive and directory you want.

3. Highlight the file to be recovered and click on the **UnErase** button.

4. Enter the first letter of the file name. The file will be automatically recovered.

• OPTIONS: FILE MENU

View Current Directory shows erased files in the current directory, including subdirectories.

View All Directories shows all erased files in all directories on the current drive.

Change Drive opens a dialog box to allow you to change drives.

Change Directory opens a dialog box containing the directory tree.

Select tags the currently highlighted file. Tagged files are recovered when you select the UnErase button.

Select Group allows you to key in a file specification. DOS wildcards "*" and "?" can be used. Press **Enter** to tag all the files matching the specification.

Unselect Group key in a file specification including DOS wildcards "*" and "?". Press **Enter** and all tagged files matching the specification will be untagged.

Rename allows you to key in a new name for the unerased file or directory.

UnErase To specifies a new drive destination for the unerased file.

Append To adds the contents of the selected file to the specified file.

For **Manual UnErase**, see *To UnErase Files Manually*.

Create File creates a new file. Use when the file is intact but its directory is missing.

• OPTIONS: SEARCH MENU

For Data Types searches the erased files looking for particular data types, such as Lotus 1-2-3 files, dBASE files, etc. Use the spacebar to toggle on your selections.

For Text allow you to enter a string of text. UnErase will search the erased files for any files that contain the string. The search is not case-sensitive.

For **For Lost Names**, see *To UnErase a File from an Erased Directory*.

Set Search Range allows you to set a starting and ending cluster number to limit the search.

Continue Search resumes a search that has been interrupted.

• OPTIONS: OPTIONS MENU

Selects the sort order for the erased files. You can sort by name, extension, time, size, directory, and prognosis. The prognosis is an indication of how likely recovery is for a particular file. The prognosis can be Excellent, Good, Average, Poor, Not Applicable, or Recovered.

You can also toggle on the option Include Nonerased Files to display all files on the selected drive, whether erased or not.

To UnErase a File from an Erased Directory

1. Start UnErase.

2. Select Search ➤ Lost Names.

3. Highlight the file you want and click on the **UnErase** button. Provide a first letter for the file name. The file will be recovered automatically.

To UnErase Files Manually

1. Start UnErase. From the File menu change to the directory where the erased files are located. Click on **View** for the list of erased files in the highlighted directory.

2. Highlight the file you want to recover and select File ➤ Manual Unerase.

3. Key in a first character for the erased file. Select **Add Cluster.**

4. Select one of the four options to add clusters to the file.

5. Click on **View File** to view the contents of the file as you go though them. Or select **View Map** to see the area on the disk occupied by the assembled clusters. Select **OK** when finished viewing.

6. Select **Save** to save the recovered file.

● OPTIONS: MANUAL UNERASE

All clusters will add all clusters likely to be part of the file.

Next probable will add only the next cluster that is probably part of the file.

Data search searches for a specific string of text.

Cluster number adds a cluster when the cluster number is known.

If you choose Data Search, key in the text and select the **Find** button in the Data Search dialog box. Toggle off **Ignore case** if you want the search to be case-sensitive. Select **Add Cluster** if you want to add the cluster containing the match to the existing file.

If you select **Cluster number**, key in the first number of the range of clusters you want to add at the Starting Cluster prompt. At the Ending Cluster prompt, key in the last number of the range. Select **OK.**

To Use UnErase from the Command Line

● SYNTAX
UNERASE (pathname) (/IMAGE) (/MIRROR) (/NOTRACK)

/IMAGE uses the Image recovery information (excludes MIRROR).

/MIRROR uses the MIRROR recovery information (excludes IMAGE).

/NOTRACK excludes Delete Tracking information.

UNFORMAT

UnFormat can recover data from a hard disk that has been formatted or damaged by a virus or power failure. UnFormat also can recover a diskette that has been formatted with Safe Format.

To UnFormat a Hard Disk

1. Insert a bootable floppy disk in drive A (it must have the same DOS version you used to format your hard disk). Reboot your system.

2. Remove the DOS diskette, insert the Fix-It Disk in drive A and key in

unformat

3. Read the message in the UnFormat dialog box and click on **Continue.**

4. Select the drive you wish to unformat and click on **OK.**

5. You will be asked if IMAGE or MIRROR was previously used to save information on the drive to be unformatted. Select **Yes** or **No,** as appropriate.

6. Select **Yes** in the confirmation box.

7. If you answered Yes in step 5 and the information has been saved, the IMAGE or MIRROR information will display. Click on **OK.** Select **Yes** in the Absolutely Sure box. Then select **Full** in the Full or Partial Restore box.

If you answered Yes in step 5 and the IMAGE or MIRROR information is not available, select **Yes** to proceed with the unformat without IMAGE or MIRROR information.

If you answered No in step 5, go on to step 8.

8. Click on **OK** once or twice, until the unformat is complete.

● **NOTE**   You can select a partial restoration in step 7: Toggle on Boot Record, File Allocation Table, or Root Directory to select these areas to be restored.

Appendix A

Installation

INSTALLING NORTON DESKTOP FOR WINDOWS

To install Norton Desktop for Windows, you will need the following hardware and software:

- IBM AT, PS/2 (286 and up) or a 100-percent compatible clone.

- A hard-disk drive with at least 8.6 Mb of free space (5.6 Mb for Version 1.0).

- 1 Mb or more of RAM (3 Mb is recommended).

- Windows 3.0 or higher.

- MS-DOS or PC-DOS, 3.1 or higher.

- A monitor that can display Windows 3.0 or higher.

A Microsoft mouse or a 100-percent compatible mouse is also recommended.

To Install Norton Desktop for Windows from DOS

1. Insert Disk No. 1 in the appropriate floppy-disk drive.

2. Key in

   a:install

   If the disk is in drive b, substitute *b:* for *a:*.

3. Follow the instructions on the screen.

To Install Norton Desktop for Windows from within Windows

1. Start Windows. Insert Disk No. 1 in the appropriate floppy-disk drive.

2. In the Program Manager select File ➤ Run.

3. In the Command Line text box, key in

   a:install

   or

   b:install

   depending on where you inserted the diskette, and click
   on **OK** or press **Enter**.

4. Follow the instructions on the screen.

To Do a Complete Installation

After following one of the procedures above, you can begin the
installation.

1. First, you will be prompted to key in both your name and
   your company's name. In order to proceed, an entry must
   be made in both text boxes. When you've finished, click on
   OK. The program will then search for a previously installed version of Norton Desktop for Windows.

2. The Install Norton Desktop Files box will open. The
   program will insert C:\NDW as the default drive and
   directory for installation in the Install To text box. The
   Target Drive Status box shows the space available on the
   drive before and after installation. To change drives, click
   on your choice in the Drives box. The Target Drive Status
   information will change to reflect the space available on
   the new drive.

3. If you do *not* want to install all of the components of
   Norton Desktop for Windows, click on the **Custom In-
   stall** button (**Select** button in Version 1.0). The Application
   Selection box will open. Click on the programs you do *not*

want to install to deselect them. Select the **OK** button
when you are finished. The Install Norton Desktop Files
window will change to show the number of applications
selected, the amount of hard-disk space required, and
the available space on the selected drive. When you
are satisfied with your choices, click on **OK**.

4. The program will open the Modify CONFIG.SYS File
dialog box to inform you that the programs requested require changes to your CONFIG.SYS file. You can choose
from one of the following options:

- **Let Install modify the config.sys file,** which will
  allow the install program to make the necessary
  changes to the config.sys file automatically. To examine or modify the changes, select the **Edit** button.
  The box will enlarge to include a screen showing
  your current CONFIG.SYS file with the changes included. Make any edits you want and click **OK**
  when you are finished.

- **Save the required changes to new file** saves
  the CONFIG.SYS file, as modified by the Install
  program, under the name *CONFIG.NEW* (or you
  can type in another file name). Your current CON-
  FIG.SYS file will not be modified in any way. Later,
  if you decide to adopt the changes, you can rename
  the CONFIG.NEW file to *CONFIG.SYS*.

- **Do not make any changes** makes no changes to
  your CONFIG.SYS.

5. The program will open the Modify AUTOEXEC.BAT File
dialog box to inform you that changes are being proposed
to your AUTOEXEC.BAT. You can choose from the same
options described under item 4, above.

6. Installation of the files will begin. You will be prompted
for additional program diskettes as they are needed.

7. A dialog box will ask you if you want to make Desktop
Editor your default Windows Text Editor (Version 2.0
only). Whatever your selection at this point, it can be
changed later by choosing Configure ➤ Default Editor.

8. A dialog box will ask if you want to schedule an automatic backup of files. If you select **Yes**, the automatic backup will be placed in the Scheduler. You will, however, still have to configure Norton Backup to perform the scheduled backup of files. If you select **No**, the automatic backup will be listed in the Scheduler's list of events, but it will not be enabled.

9. You will then be asked if you want to make Norton Desktop your Windows shell. If you select **Yes**, the install program will make the necessary changes automatically in the SYSTEM.INI file. Using Norton Desktop as your shell will save Windows memory. Note that the Program Manager files are neither deleted nor changed, but they are removed from view. If you select **No**, be sure to minimize the Program Manager while you are running Norton Desktop.

10. If changes were made to your AUTOEXEC.BAT or CONFIG.SYS file, choose **Reboot** from the Installation Complete window. If no changes were made, select Restart Windows.

● **NOTE**   If you do not install all the Norton Desktop programs and wish to add them later, you can run the Install program again. At that time select only the desired additional programs from the Application Selection dialog box.

UNINSTALL

After using Norton Desktop for a while, you may want to remove tools or utilities that you don't use. You can also uninstall Norton Desktop as your shell and return to the Windows Program Manager. Anything you remove can be recovered by running the Install program again. Uninstall is available in Version 2.0 only.

To Uninstall Norton Desktop for Windows

1. Open the Norton Desktop Applications window. Double-click on the Norton Desktop Uninstall icon. A window will open informing you that the uninstall program needs to take control of the environment. If you have applications open, you should close them before proceeding. If you want to go ahead, click on **OK**.

2. The next dialog box presents you with radio buttons to select one of the following options

- Remove Norton Desktop as the Windows Shell
- Select Features to Remove
- Completely Remove Norton Desktop for Windows

3. If you choose to select features to remove, another dialog box will open showing the location for the Norton Desktop files. If the path is incorrect, type in the new path. Click on **OK**.

4. The next dialog box will list the parts of the desktop and the amount of hard-disk space occupied by each part. By default, all are selected. Click on **Deselect All** and then click on the ones you want to remove. When only the ones you want to remove are highlighted, click on **OK**.

5. The program will complete the uninstall process.

Appendix B

Configuring the Desktop in Version 1.0

THE BUTTON BAR

The button bar at the bottom of Drive Windows can be omitted by deselecting the Display Button Bar box in the Configure Button Bar window, or it can be edited in various ways.

By default, the buttons that appear on the button bar are the following:

- Move
- Copy
- Delete
- View Pane
- Type Sort
- Name Sort

To Change the Button Command

1. Select Configure ➤ Button Bar.

2. Find the command you want on the Menu Item list and select it using the mouse.

3. Click the button to which you want the command assigned.

4. Select **OK** when you are finished. To make the change permanent, choose Configure ➤ Save Configuration or the Save Configuration on Exit checkbox in the Preferences dialog box (Configure ➤ Preferences).

● **NOTE**   Select commands carefully. For example, the Menu Item list includes two items named *All*. One is from the Select menu and the other from the Deselect menu. Even though their names are the same, their functions are exactly opposite.

See Also   *Saving the Configuration*

To Edit the Text on Buttons

1.   Select the Edit button in the Configure Button Bar dialog box.

2.   In the Edit Button Bar dialog box, click on the text box of the button you want to modify and key in the text. The program will beep if you attempt to enter too much text.

3.   Click on **OK** when you are finished.

● **NOTE**   Take care not to change the meaning of the button. Changing the text on the button changes only its appearance. The function of the button can be changed only by selecting another Menu Item in the Configure Button Bar window.

CONFIRMATION REQUESTS

You can take many actions in Norton Desktop for Windows—some of which you may later regret. To protect yourself from various types of hasty actions, you can toggle on the display of dialog boxes that will ask for confirmation of the action to be taken.

To Be Prompted for File Names

1.   Select Configure ➤ Preferences.

2.   From the Prompt for Filename box, choose the operations for which you would like a prompt.

3.   Click on **OK** when you are finished.

• **NOTE** The Prompt for Filename option works when you first
select one or more files from a Drive Window and then choose the
Edit, View, Print, or Delete functions. It is a precaution that allows
you to change your mind before taking an action. If you don't want
to be prompted, clear some or all of the check boxes.

To Select Confirmation Requests

You can choose to have dialog boxes pop up and ask for confirmation when certain potentially "dangerous" operations (such as
deleting files) are attempted. To do so, follow these steps:

1. Select Configure ➤ Confirmation.

2. Click on the confirmation options you want.

3. Click **OK** when you are finished.

● **OPTIONS**

A **Delete** warning appears when you are deleting an unprotected file. If Erase Protect is on, the warning message will
not appear, but you will still be asked to confirm the deletion.

A **Subtree Delete** warning appears for any operation involving the removal of a directory.

A **Replace** warning appears for any copy operation that involves overwriting another file. This box should *remain checked*, because if you write over a file, the file will be lost and will not be
recoverable by any means.

Mouse Operation opens a confirmation dialog box for all
mouse operations that move, copy, or delete files.

An **Unformatted Print** warning appears when you try to print
a file for which there is no associated application. This will appear whether you've used File ➤ Print File or dragged the file
from a Drive Window to the Desktop Printer Icon.

CONTROL MENUS

Control menus are menus that appear when you click once on a desktop icon or on the control box in the upper-left corner of application windows. An application window's Control menu can be configured. The desktop icon's menu can only be turned on or off.

To Configure the Control Box Menus

1. Choose Configure ➤ Preferences.

2. The Control Menu check boxes are in the lower-left corner of the Preferences dialog box. Select any of the items you want to appear on the menus.

3. Click on **OK** when you are finished. Your selections will be available from the control box on any application window.

To Turn on the Drive/Tool Icon Control Menu

1. Select Configure ➤ Preferences.

2. Click on the Drive/Tool Icon Control Menu check box.

3. Click **OK**.

● MENU OPTIONS

Click once on a drive icon or desktop icon to see the Control menu.

Open opens the drive or starts the program.

Icon allows you to select another icon.

Label opens a dialog box where you can change the label that appears under the icon.

Close closes the drive or program and removes the icon from the desktop.

DESKTOP ICONS

Icons on the desktop represent either a program or a file with its associated program. The appearance of icons can be changed by selecting from the icons available in Norton Desktop for Windows or by designing your own icons using the Icon Editor.

To Select Tool Icons

1. Choose Configure ➤ Preferences.

2. In the Tool Icons box, check the boxes for the icons you want to appear on the desktop when Norton Desktop for Windows starts. If you have more than one printer, click on the Printers button to choose the printer that you want associated with the Printer Icon. Up to four printers, including a fax machine, can be selected; each printer will have its own icon.

3. When you have made your selections, click on **OK**.

● **NOTE**   To reduce desktop clutter, you do not have to create an icon for every printer you might want to use. The full Printer Selection box is also available when you select File ➤ Print.

To Change an Icon Label

1. Click once on the desktop icon.

2. Choose Label from the pop-up menu.

3. Key in the label you want to appear on the icon.

4. Select **OK** when you are finished.

● **NOTE**   The Drive/Tool Icon Control Menu option must be switched on to change the icon or the icon label. This check-box item is available in the Preferences dialog box (Configure ➤ Preferences).

To Change a Desktop Icon

1. Click once on the desktop icon.

2. Select Icon from the pop-up menu.

3. The Choose Icon dialog box opens as shown in Figure B.1. The Icon File text box shows the path for the current icon. Click on the prompt button to see a list of the file names and paths of your most recent choices. The Icon(s) box shows the current icon. Click on the Icon's prompt button to see all the icons available in the current path.

4. Choose an icon from the Icon(s) box. If the icon you want is not in the selected path, click on the Browse button.

5. Highlight the source file you want and click **OK**. To see the icons in the source file, select the View button.

6. Scroll up and down the Icon(s) box to find the icon you want. Highlight the icon and click **OK**. The highlighted icon will be transferred to the Desktop icon automatically.

● **NOTE**   The source files for icons will have one of four extensions: .ICO, .NIL, .EXE, or .DLL. Therefore, the Browse box will show only files with these extensions. However, not all files with these extensions will have icons in them. If you select a new source file, click the View button, and the icon does not change, it means that the selected file contains no icons.

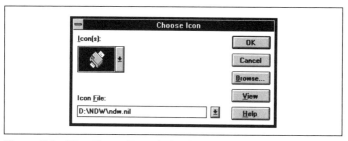

Figure B.1: The Choose Icon dialog box

DRIVE WINDOWS

Drive Windows are at the heart of Norton Desktop for Windows. They replace the Windows File Manager by allowing you to copy, move, delete, view, and find files with a button click or two. By default, the Drive Window buttons appear on the left side of the desktop and include all available drives, including networked drives; but, like most things in Norton Desktop for Windows, this is configurable.

To Configure the Drive Icons

1. Select Configure ➤ Drive Icons.

2. Use the mouse to highlight the individual drive icons.

3. If you also want to specify All Hard Disks, All Network Drives, or All Floppy Drives, click on the appropriate check boxes in Drive Types.

4. To display the drive icons, click on the check box and select a radio button to choose the display location.

5. Select **OK** to confirm the choices or **Cancel** to return to the previous configuration.

To Open a Drive Window

To open a Drive Window, double-click on the drive icon on the Desktop or select Window ➤ Open Drive Window. You can have more than one Drive Window for the same drive open at the same time, and windows for more than one drive can also be open simultaneously.

THE PARTS OF A DRIVE WINDOW

The various parts of the Drive Window work together to make it easy to do most file operations with a click or two. The components of the Drive Window are listed below.

Status Bar displays information about the drive, directory, or file(s) selected.

Drive Selector is a combination box that allows you to change drives without opening up another Drive Window. To change drives, highlight this box and key in the letter of the drive or click on the drop-down box prompt button and select the drive.

Button Bar has up to six buttons that can be configured to whatever file functions you use most often. By default, these are Move, Copy, Delete, View Pane, Type Sort, and Name Sort. To modify these settings, see *Part Two, The Button Bar.*

Copy, Move, and **Delete** all work in a similar manner. To copy a file, highlight the file or files in the File Pane and then click on the Copy button. This opens up the Copy dialog box. Key in the destination to the Destination combination box or select the prompt button to pull down a list of recent destinations. Alternatively, you can pick the Select button to open an enhanced dialog box. When the Destination box is correct, select **OK** to confirm the copy or **Cancel** to abandon the change.

Type Sort toggles the display to show the files sorted by extension.

View Pane opens the View Pane. Click on it again to close the View Pane. The View Pane should not be confused with the Viewer, which also allows you to view files, but which is more versatile.

Name Sort toggles the display to show the files sorted by file name.

Panes make up the main body of the Drive Window. They display the selected drive's tree structure, a file list, and optionally (with View Pane toggled on) the contents of the currently selected file.

A **Speed Search Box** is the quickest way to find a file or directory in either the Tree Pane or the File Pane. Note that you must start keying in characters for the Speed Search box to appear. When you begin keying in the name of the file or directory, the Speed Search box appears below the appropriate pane and the cursor bar moves to highlight the first file or directory that matches the keyed-in letters. When the cursor bar has moved to the file or directory you want, press **Enter** to select it.

If the Tree Pane is active, the Speed Search box works in the Tree Pane. If the File Pane is active, the Speed Search box works there. Press **Tab** to cycle the pane highlighter through the drive selecter, Tree Pane, File Pane, and button bar.

To Refresh the Drive Windows

The display of files and directories in the Drive Windows does not always update automatically as moves, deletions, and so forth, are made. To update the display, select View ➤ Refresh or press **F5**.

To Configure the Panes

From the View menu, select from the following:

➤ **Tree Pane** to toggle the Tree Pane on and off.

➤ **File Pane** to toggle the File Pane on and off.

➤ **View Pane** to toggle the View Pane on and off.

➤ **Show Entire Drive** to replace the Tree and File Panes with a pane showing all the files on the drive and their locations.

To Filter the File Display in the File Pane

1. Select View ➤ Filter to bring up the Filter dialog box.

2. From the list in the File Type box, select the file types to display:

   • Select All Files to show all the files.

   • Select Programs to show all executable programs (.COM, .EXE, .BAT, and .PIF).

   • Select Documents to show all document files (.DOC, .WRI, .TXT).

   • Select Custom to define a custom filter.

3. If you chose Custom, fill in the combination box with the file specification(s) that you want displayed or choose from a list of recent selections. (Note that Custom can be used with wildcards in the file specifications.)

4. From the Attributes box, choose which files to display by attribute.

5. Select **OK** to confirm the choices or **Cancel** to return to the previous configuration.

● EXAMPLES

- Toggle the Hidden attribute to blank to exclude hidden files.

- Toggle the Archive attribute to gray to see files regardless of whether they have been backed up or not.

- Choose Custom, then key in ***.W??** to see all Lotus and Quattro Pro spreadsheet files.

- Choose Custom, then key in ***.XLS *.W??** to see all spread-sheet files, including Excel files.

To Change the File Pane Detail

1. Select View ➤ File Details to bring up the File Details dialog box.

2. Select the File options that you want to see displayed in the File Pane. Items marked with an *X* will show in the pane. The sample line shows how the files will appear.

3. Select **OK** to confirm the choices or **Cancel** to return to the previous configuration.

● OPTIONS

Icons toggles the display of file icons. An icon for a text file resembles a page with lines of writing on it. Executable files, such as programs and batch files, have icons that resemble onscreen windows. All other files have icons that look like a blank page of paper.

Date toggles the inclusion of the file creation date in the display.

Attributes toggles whether the file display includes the file attributes (Hidden, System, Read Only, or Archive).

Size toggles the inclusion of the file size in the display.

Time toggles whether the file creation time is included in the display.

Directory toggles the display of the file's directory. (Active only in Show Entire Drive mode.)

To Change the Sort Order in the File Pane

1. Select View ➤ Sort By.

2. Use the mouse to highlight the file characteristic by which to sort or select Ascending or Descending sort order. The display will be updated immediately.

● **OPTIONS**

Name sorts alphabetically by file name.

Type sorts alphabetically by file extension.

Size sorts by file size.

Date sorts by file creation date and time.

Unsorted displays files in DOS order.

Ascending displays files in alphabetical order, smallest to largest, or most recent to oldest.

Descending displays files in reverse alphabetical order, largest to smallest, or oldest to most recent.

● **NOTES** By default, the primary sort order is by file name. If type, size, or date is chosen as the primary sort, then the secondary sort is by name. The default sort is performed in ascending order (*A* before *Z*, *1980* before *1991*, small before large) unless descending order is checked.

EDITOR

Any Editor program can be used to edit files in response to the File ➤ Edit command. The default editor is Notepad.

To Set a New Default Editor

1. Select Configure ➤ Editor.

2. Key in the full path of the editor program that you want to use. If you don't know the exact name of the program, click on the Browse button. Highlight the name of the editor and then select **OK**. The editor name will be returned to the Editor Program text box.

3. Then select **OK** again to save the new default editor.

LAUNCH FUNCTIONS

The Launch Manager and Launch List are located in all the control box menus generated inside Norton Desktop for Windows. Using Launch, you can open a file and its associated application from virtually anywhere in Norton Desktop for Windows. When you launch an application or script, it executes. When you open a document file, its associated application executes and the file opens. If the file is not associated with an application, the result will be an error message.

To Configure the Launch Manager

1. Select Launch Manager from any control box menu.

2. To add a menu item, click **Add**. In the Text box, key in the name of the item as you want it to appear on the Launch List. If you want to add an Alt-key accelerator to this command, place an ampersand (&) just before the accelerator's letter.

3.   In the Command Line box, key in the path for the item.

4.   To associate a shortcut key combination with the item, key in a two-key combination of **Shift**, **Alt**, or **Ctrl** and any second key. If you want the menu listing to show the shortcut key, click on the check box. Select **OK** twice to confirm the addition.

● OPTIONS

Edit: use the mouse to highlight a menu item and select **Edit** to modify any item on the menu.

Delete: highlight the item and then click **Delete** to remove the item from the Launch List.

Move Up/Move Down: highlight a menu item and then click on **Move Up** or **Move Down**: to change an item's position on the Launch List.

To Launch a File from the Launch Manager

1.   Pull down the control box menu anywhere in Norton Desktop for Windows.

2.   Highlight Launch List and a list of launchable programs/documents will drop down.

3.   Select the desired item and the application will execute.

To Launch a File from a File Pane

1.   Select Window ➤ Open Drive Window or double-click on the appropriate drive icon.

2.   Double-click on the filename in the Drive Window.

To Launch a File from a Group Window

Double-click on the selected icon in its Group Window.

To Launch a File from a File Icon

1. Open the appropriate Drive Window and select the file from the file list.

2. Drag the file's icon to the name of the application on the list. This name must have an .EXE or .COM extension. The application will execute and the file will open.

Note that before the application executes, a Warning message appears:

Are you sure you want to start *application* **using** *filename* **as the initial file?**

Answer **Yes**.

● **NOTE**   This procedure can also be used to open files not associated with an application. In addition, it will work with a file that has an extension associated with a different application than the one you want to use. However, if you drag the file to an application icon on the desktop, the file will not open, and the file icon will remain on the desktop until you close it.

To Launch a File from the Command Line

1. Select File ➤ Run.

2. If the file is associated with an application, key in the file name and extension only. If the file does not have an association with an application, key in the full path.

● **OPTIONS**

For **Previous launches**, select the prompt box next to the Run Window's Command Line text box and a list will appear of the last ten applications launched.

Normal applications will launch in their normal configuration.

Minimized when selected, causes an application to shrink to icon size automatically as soon as it is launched.

Maximized causes launched files to appear full screen on your desktop.

Browse allows you to search through all drives and directories to select applications and files.

MENUS

By default, the Norton Desktop menu bar starts with short menus that contain only the most commonly used commands. All commands are listed in the full menus, which are reached by choosing Configure ➤ Full Menus.

The menus and the menu bar are not static. You can add new menus and redesign existing menus in any way that suits you. If you specify a password, only users who know it will be able to get to the full custom menus.

When you select Configure ➤ Edit Custom Menus, you will see the Menu Assignments dialog box, as shown in Figure B.2.

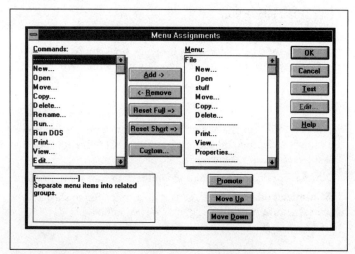

Figure B.2: The Menu Assignments dialog box

To Add a Function to an Existing Menu

1. Choose Configure ➤ Edit Custom Menus.

2. Scroll through the Command list and highlight the command you want. When you pick an item, a brief description of its function will appear in the lower-left corner of the dialog box.

3. In the Menu List box, highlight the item that you want to directly follow the new function.

4. Click on the **Add** button and the new command will be inserted right above the highlighted menu item.

5. Click **OK**.

• **NOTE**   If you do not highlight a menu item, the Add function will not work.

To Delete a Menu Item

1. Select Configure ➤ Edit Custom Menus.

2. Highlight the item you want to delete in the Menu box.

3. Click **Remove**. The item will be deleted.

4. Click on **OK** to exit the dialog box.

To Make a Custom Menu

1. Select Configure ➤ Edit Custom Menus.

2. Click on the **Custom** button in the Menu Assignments dialog box.

3. In the Type of item box, click on the radio button for New Menu.

4. Key in the title for the menu in the Text box.

5. Click **OK** when you are finished.

6. To preview the results, click the **Test** button in the Menu Assignments box to see what the new menu will look like.

The title will appear as the left-most menu in the menu bar. Use the control box menu to close the menu Test window.

7. Click **OK** when you are finished.

● **NOTE**   To include an Alt-*key* accelerator in the menu name, key in an ampersand (&) directly in front of the accelerator letter. For example, key in *&Sales* and the menu will be highlighted when you enter the Alt-S key combination.

To Create a Custom Menu Item

1. Select Configure ➤ Edit Custom Menus.

2. Click on the **Custom** button in the Menu Assignments dialog box.

3. Under Type of item, click on the radio button for New Command.

4. In the Text box, key in the name of the item as you want it to appear in the menu.

5. Key in the name of the program, script, or file that you want to launch when this menu item is selected. The Command line must either be the complete path for the program to be launched or a file name with an associated extension.

6. If you want a shortcut key, enter the key or key combination in the Shortcut Key text box. Click on the check box if you want the shortcut key to display in the menu listing.

7. Click **OK**. Preview the menu by clicking on the **Test** button.

8. Select **OK** again when you are finished.

To Edit a Standard Menu Item

1. Select Configure ➤ Edit Custom Menus. The Menu Assignments dialog box will open.

2. Highlight the Menu item you wish to edit and click on the **Edit** button to open the Edit Menu Text Item dialog box.

3. In the Text box, key in the name as you want it to appear on the menu. Include an ampersand (&) directly in front of the letter that you want underlined.

4. Key in a shortcut key, if you want one, and click on the check box if you want the shortcut key to show in the menu.

5. The original setting for the item is shown at the top of the dialog box. Click on the **Original** button if you want to restore it. Select **OK** when you are finished.

To Edit a Customized Menu Item

1. Select Configure ➤ Edit Custom Menus.

2. In the Menu Assignments dialog box, highlight the custom menu item you want to edit, then click on the **Edit** button. The Edit Customized Menu Item dialog box will open.

3. Edit the menu item.

4. Click on **OK** when finished or **Cancel** to abandon the operation.

To Change the Order of Menu Items

1. Open the Menu Assignments dialog box by selecting Configure ➤ Edit Custom Menus.

2. Using the scroll bar on the Menu box, highlight the item that you want to move.

    *   To move the item up one position, click on the **Move Up** button.
    *   To move the item down one position, click on the **Move Down** button.
    *   To promote an item up though the menu hierarchy, highlight it and click on the **Promote** button. To demote the item, click on the **Move Down** button.

3. Use the **Test** button to view the menu you have constructed. Close the Menu Test box.

4. Click on **OK** when you are finished.

● **NOTE**   Items can also be moved up and down by clicking on them and then dragging them to the position you want.

Names that are flush left in the Menu list are menu bar items. Indented under these are items directly under a menu title. The next indentation is for items in a cascaded menu.

To Remove a Menu or Menu Item

1.   Select Configure ➤ Edit Custom Menus.

2.   In the Menu box, highlight the item you want to remove.

3.   Click on the **Remove** button. If you pick a single command, it will be deleted without further warning. If you choose a menu, a warning box will open advising you that the menu and all the items below it will be deleted if you proceed.

4.   Make your choice and click **OK** when the deletion is finished.

To Restore Original Menus

If you decide either to rebuild your custom menus or to abandon them completely, you can easily reset the Short or Full Menus to their original configurations.

1.   Select Configure ➤ Edit Custom Menus.

2.   To reset the menu to the default Full Menus, choose Reset Full. To reset to Short Menus, choose Reset Short.

3.   Click on **OK** when you are finished.

PASSWORDS

If a password dialog box appears, it means that you have entered an area where a password is required. Passwords can be maintained for two different areas:

- Custom menus: Passwords can be set to prevent users from accessing certain menu commands. This type of password is set using Configure ➤ Password.

- Quick Access: Passwords can restrict the use of groups or objects in Quick Access.

To Set a Menu Password

1. Select Configure ➤ Password.

2. Key in the password that you want in the Password text box. The password, which can be up to twenty characters long, appears as asterisks (*) to ensure privacy.

3. Press **OK** and a Confirm Password box will appear. Key in the password a second time and choose **OK** again.

Note that once a password has been set and you choose Configure ➤ Short Menus to switch to Short Menus, you will need the password to return to Full Menus.

To Maintain a Password in Quick Access

1. For a new item, select Password in the New dialog box.

2. For an existing item, select Password from the Properties dialog box.

3. In the Password text box, key in any combination of letters and numbers up to twenty characters long. The password appears as a series of asterisks (*) to keep anyone from seeing it as you key it in. Click on **OK**.

4. You will be asked to confirm the password by keying it in again. After you key in the password a second time, press **Enter** or select **OK**. Note that if the second password entry does not match the first, no password will be set.

● **NOTE**   To make the password permanent, you must choose Configure ➤ Save Configuration or check the Save Configuration on Exit check box in the Preferences dialog box (Configure ➤ Preferences).

Otherwise, the password is in effect only for the current session of
Norton Desktop for Windows.

To Remove a Menu Password

1.   Select Configure ➤ Password.

2.   First, you will be asked for the current password. Key it in
     the Password text box and choose **OK**.

3.   In the Enter New Password dialog box, key in the new
     password and click on **OK**. If you want no password,
     press the **Enter** key.

4.   The next box will ask you to confirm the password or to
     confirm that you don't want a password. Either key in the
     new password and click on **OK**, or press **Enter** to confirm
     that you want no password.

SAVING THE
CONFIGURATION

Changes in Edit Custom Menus, Shortcut Keys, SmartErase, and
Launch List will be saved automatically, but you must use one of the
save methods for other changes to be made permanent. The two
methods have some overlapping functions, but they are not identical.

To Save the Appearance of Your Desktop

This method will preserve the appearance of your desktop as you
leave it.

1.   Select Configure ➤ Preferences.

2.   Check the Save Configuration on Exit box.

3.   Click on **OK** when you are finished. When you next start
     Norton Desktop for Windows, the desktop will be as it
     was when you left it.

To Restart with a Standard Desktop

Arrange the desktop the way you want it to appear when you next start Norton Desktop for Windows. Click on Configure ➤ Save Configuration. Note that the desktop will continue to re-open with this appearance until the next time you choose Configure ➤ Save Configuration.

SHORTCUT KEYS

With shortcut keys, you can choose menu commands without opening a menu. Setting the shortcut keys for your commonly used functions can save you time and keystrokes.

To Assign a Shortcut Key

1. Select Configure ➤ Shortcut Keys. The Configure Shortcut Keys dialog box opens.

2. All the commands available in the default Full Menus are in the Menu Item box. Scroll though the box until you find the command you want. Highlight the command.

3. In the New Key text box, key in the shortcut key that you want assigned to this command. Use the actual key-strokes. If you use an invalid key combination, the program will refuse it.

4. If you want the shortcut key to appear in the menu next to the command, check the box next to the Include key name option in the standard menu.

5. Click **OK** when you are finished.

These are the keys you can use for shortcut keys:

- Any function key except **F1** (F1 reserved for Help).

- Any combination of **Shift** plus a function key (except F1).

- A combination of the **Ctrl** key and any function key, number, letter, or direction key.

- A combination of **Ctrl** and **Shift** and any function key, number, letter, or direction key.

- A combination of **Alt** with either **Shift** or **Ctrl** plus a function key, number, letter, or direction key.

● **NOTE**   You can use the numbers at the top of the keyboard and the numbers on the numeric keypad as different numbers. For example, Ctrl-8 using the number *8* from the regular keyboard is a different shortcut key from Ctrl-8 using the numeric keypad *8*.

VIEW FILES

The Viewer will display a file according to the file's extension. For example, .DOC indicates a file written in Microsoft Word. If the file lacks an extension, the Viewer will display the file according to the default setting. For a list of the default choices, open the Viewer and select Viewer ➤ Set Default Viewer.

If you have a TIFF graphics image file, for example, without an extension or with an extension that does not identify it as a TIFF file, you will not be able to view the file unless the Viewer's default setting is TIFF (Grayscale and Color).

To View a File

1. Double-click on the Viewer desktop icon or the File Viewer icon in the Norton Desktop Group Window. The Norton Viewer window will pop up on your desktop.

2. Select File ➤ Open.

3. Choose the file you want to view from the Browse box. Click **OK**. The file will appear in its own window inside the Viewer window.

4. Repeat steps 1 and 2 to view additional files. You can also double-click on the file name in the Open File window that appears.

● **SHORTCUT** Click on the file in an open Drive Window and drag it to the Viewer desktop icon.

● **OPTIONS: FILE MENU**

Open opens a Browse window, where you can select a file to view.

Close closes the file in the active window.

Exit closes the File Viewer window.

● **OPTIONS: VIEWER MENU**

Set Default Viewer changes the translator for the next file you select to view. If the file has an extension recognized as the default by Norton Desktop, it will be opened in the recognized format. If not, the program will attempt to open the file in the translation specified here.

Set Current Viewer changes the file translation for the active window. For example, if you have a text file in the active window, select Hex Dump to see the file in a hexadecimal translation.

● **OPTIONS: SEARCH MENU**

Find searches for a text string or data that you specify. Key in the characters you want to search for and click **OK**. The program will search the active window for that string and stop when it is found.

Find Next searches for the next occurrence of the string specified.

Find Previous searches backward in the active window for the previous occurrence of the specified string.

GoTo brings up the GoTo dialog box when you are viewing a spreadsheet or database, to let you input a specific row and column or field and record for the program to find.

• OPTIONS: WINDOW MENU

Cascade arranges the open file windows in stair-steps with the title bars showing and the active file on top.

Tile arranges the open windows so that all are visible. The amount of space allotted to each window diminishes as the number of open files increases.

Arrange Icons adjusts the positions of the icons in minimized file windows.

Close All closes all the open file windows but leaves the Viewer window open.

● **NOTE**   At the bottom of this menu there is a list of all the open files with a checkmark designating the active window. If you have more than nine files open, click on More Windows to see a complete list. When you click on More Windows, the Select Window appears, with a drop-down list inside. You can double-click on the file name to make it active, or highlight the file name and select **OK**. To make another file the active window, use the mouse to select it.

Index